Kiwese

Alex Buzo was born in Sydney and educated at the University of NSW. He has been one of Australia's leading authors for many years and his works include *The Marginal Farm* (set in Fiji), *Macquarie* (set in colonial Australia), *Prue Flies North* (set in Queensland), *Makassar Reef* (set in Indonesia) and *Tautology* (set in hardened concrete) as well as *Norm and Ahmed*, *Coralie Lansdowne Says No*, and *The Longest Game*, a book on Australasian cricket which he co-edited with Jamie Grant.

Also by **Alex Buzo**

Kiwese

A Guide
A Ductionary
A Shearing of Unsights

Alex Buzo

MANDARIN

Published 1994 by Mandarin
a part of Reed Books Australia
22 Salmon Street, Port Melbourne, Victoria 3207
a division of Reed International Books Australia Pty Limited

Typeset in Garamond no. 3 by Bookset Pty Ltd
Printed and bound in Australia by McPherson's Printing Group

National Library of Australia
  cataloguing-in-publication data:

Buzo, Alexander, 1944-   .
  Kiwise.

  ISBN 1 86330 342 1.

  I. English language—Spoken English—New Zealand—Dictionaries. 2.
  English language—Spoken English—New Zealand—Humor. 3.
  English language—Spoken English—Australia—Dictionaries. 4. English
  language—Spoken English—Australia—Humor. 5. Pleonasm. I. Title.

427.993

Dedicated to
Perce P. Cassidy

Author's note

There is no guarantee that the reader of this book will automatically be able to speak Kiwese. In romantic Auckland, where to live is 'to love' or festive Wellington, where children are sent home with 'nuts' in their hair, it takes years of practice to sound like that. All I can offer is an exploration of Antipodean idioms and the hope that knowledge will bring understanding.

The Shaky Isles

Auckland

Bay of Plinty

New Plum-mouth

Guzborn

Terror Necky
(provunce)

Den O'vehic

Nilsson

Willington

Blinnum

N

Dunedun

Unver Cargle

The Land of Oz

Introduction

1976 was a dud year. Australia won two bronze medals at the Montreal Olympics, Jimmy Carter was elected US President, and a media executive told me there was no such thing as a New Zealand accent. Accordingly, he cut a whole character and several jokes out of a script I had written for his television series.

The executive's surname was not Crusoe, but it might have been Burchfield. Dr Robert Burchfield, Chief Editor of the *Oxford English Dictionary*, asserted in *The Story of English* that 'if a New Zealander and an Australian from the same social background shared a railway carriage only an expert phonetician could tell them apart on the basis of pronunciation'.

What on earth are these people talking about?

Kiwese

It is obvious to anyone who has visited the Kiwi
enclaves of Bondi, St Kilda and Cairns that New
Zealanders have a strong, identifiable accent and a
distinctive expatriate culture. Anyone sitting in
a railway carriage going from Bondi to Edgecliff
who does not recognise the lilting tones of Kiwese
could only be a television producer or an 'expert
phonetician'.

Of course, not everyone has come into contact
with Kiwese; in a bakery shop in Bondi the
woman being served just before me asked, 'How
much are the rolls?' 'Tin since,' came the reply
from the customary Kiwi behind the counter. 'Er
. . . ten cents?' queried the woman, with just a
hint of translation. 'Yiss!' came the confident reply.
Recognising that not everyone is familiar with
the Kiwi accent, Channel Nine thoughtfully
supplied English subtitles for a story from the Shaky
Isles on its six o'clock news. This book is intended
to provide further enlightenment.

Since 1976 there have been a few grudging
acknowledgements that a New Zealand accent does
exist. Most of these public confessors are New
Zealand expatriates, and most of them insist that
any accent that is now discernible is only a recent
phenomenon. In this context it is interesting to

note that Clarrie Grimmett, who played Test cricket for Australia from 1925 to 1936, was called 'Grum' by his team-mates as an affectionate tribute to his New Zealand birth and accent.

When I visited Auckland in 1993 I taped conversations with several older Kiwis and found their accent was, if anything, even 'thucker' than their younger compatriots. They say 'must' for mist, 'injun' for engine, and 'sneer' for snare — all leading characteristics of Kiwese. Indeed, a senior Kiwi described Auckland as 'the suttee of sails'.

One veteran expatriate holds a view that does not mark him out as Robinson Crusoe. He contends that there was no En Zed accent until all their vowels were suddenly sucked away 'about twenty years ago'. When I was in New Zealand I discovered that they had plenty of vowels; they just use them in different places. 'En Zed' is pronounced 'In Zid', and as for the exclusive store Sak's, well, a clerk in the duty free booth at the airport told me that she represented 'Sex'.

There are of course many motives for the many people who have denied the existence of Kiwese. Some NZ grandees tried to suppress any talk about an indigenous accent, believing that they sounded not only English, but like members of the aristocracy, which they pronounced, in reality, 'mimbers of the error stock racey'.

Academics, too, have a history of denying the culture and accent of Australasia. Professor J.I.M. Stewart of Adelaide University stated in 1940 that there was no Australian literature worthy of study, while Professor John Bernard stated in 1981 that there was no regional variation in Australian English. These were sincerely and widely held views, and I think it is cynical to suggest that academics have suppressed their knowledge of Antipodean idioms so they can secure overseas travel grants. I believe it is simply a case of incompetence. These people have such tin ears that they cannot recognise the simplest regional variation in Australia, let alone New Zealand.

One thing I have not attempted is a guide to NZ regions, as the Kiwese rendered here is more the language of the expatriate culture. Anyone interested in the subject could make a start by listening to the ABC's Otago correspondent and trying to identify what it is that she is saying.

The book is a dictionary, a celebration of what is distinctive about the Kiwese language as a whole, rendered in what I hope is a fair and accurate manner. Do they say 'Ruchard Kumble' for Richard

Kimble? Is Kim Campbell pronounced 'Come
Kemble'? And is Red Adair really 'Rid a Dear'?
Well, not quite, but that's about as close as you can
get without descending into phonetics.

Why compile such a dictionary? There are many
dutiful colonials who believe that it is more
important to consume cultural idioms from overseas
rather than try to make sense of our own. I have
to confess to being at odds with these good people
and have set, as one of my goals, the idea that
you can make sense of this part of the world. In
Macquarie I dealt with the early years of New South
Wales, in *Prue Flies North* the later years of
Queensland, in *The Marginal Farm* with colonial
Fiji and in *Makassar Reef* with post-colonial
Indonesia. In part, this has been an attempt to
rectify the bias of my education, which had plenty
about Joan of Arc but very little on the
Asia–Pacific region and certainly nothing about its
history and infinite variety.

In recent years Australia has tried — with some
success — to break out of the 'dutiful colonial'
mode. Professional Australians such as Paul Hogan
have stamped the Australian idiom on the rest
of the world, so much so that every American now
wants to try out a Hogan-inspired 'Orcy' accent

on every Australian who visits America. Hogan's television commercials, in which he urged Americans to come to Australia and 'put a shrimp on the barbie' were a great success and made Australia 'flavour of the month', as they say in all the show-biz bibles. When I was last in America I mentioned I had just come from New Zealand and was received with blank looks. The rest of the world has very little idea about New Zealand's vigorous culture and idiom; there are no professional New Zealanders doing a Hogan.

In the northern hemisphere the expatriate Kiwi tends to be a chameleon, and you will find them reading the news on radio and television throughout the English-speaking world. In every case they sound exactly like everyone else around them. Many Kiwis have realised the dream of migrating to England and, after some strenuous work, being taken for a native of the British Isles. Some even go in for what I call Reverse Kiwese, a process in which the shedding of the accent goes too far. If a normal inhabitant of the Shakies calls Sting 'Stung', then an overseas chameleon will say 'Samsing' for Samsung.

The Kiwi expatriate community of Australia is largely Kiwese-speaking, very noticeable, and increasingly the victim of Kiwi-bashing. In 1983, when England played New Zealand in a cricket match at Adelaide Oval, I estimated the crowd support at 45 per cent for England and noted the phenomenon in a newspaper article. At the time I attributed it to Adelaide's Anglophilia, and was disappointed that the crowd was not unequivocally behind New Zealand (population three million) as opposed to England (population fifty million) on the grounds of underdoghood, if not Anzac solidarity. How wrong can you be! By 1992 New Zealand attracted less than 20 per cent crowd support and were booed on to the field during the World Series and Bledisloe Cup matches. Songs such as 'As Long As We Beat New Zealand' became standards. The 1983 game in Adelaide revealed a growing antipathy to the Land of the Long White Cloud, and misunderstandings about their expatriate culture must be held at least partly responsible.

The Irish diaspora sent forth James Joyce to Paris. The Jewish diaspora gave Lillian Hellman to New York. The Kiwi diaspora, or 'duspersal' has been, per capita, the richest of all. Australian television screens have been illuminated by a galaxy of the brightest stars — Jack Davey, Dinah Lee,

Brian Henderson, David Low, Pamela Stevenson, Bruno Lawrence, Derryn Hinch and Bruce Spence (not his real name). Oz Lit has also been propped up by Ruth Park, Douglas Stewart, Olaf Ruhen, Jane Galletly, John Sligo, Jennifer Compton, Max Richards and Rosie Scott. Where would Oz politics be without Sir Joh Bjelke-Petersen or 'Jumpin' Jack' Fahey? Fred Hollows, Tim Elliott and Kurt Sorensen, Ricky May and Kiri te Kanawa, Kerry Fox, Sam Neill and Bruce Judge, John Clarke, Terry Clarke, Sir Ron Brierley and Valerie 'The Editor' Lawson — the list goes on. Is it the most significant movement of peoples in the modern era? It must be pretty close to it, and this book is a long-overdue tribute.

However much I may personally deplore the rift ('roughed' in Kiwese) in trans-Tasman relations, I am bound to record it, as writers who shy away from the truth cannot hope to gain a place in any sort of pantheon. There is much that is positive in the vigour and invention of Kiwese, much to be celebrated, too, and this must also be taken into account, along with the inevitable jokes about sheep, wet towels, and 'six'.

New Zealand is not mentioned in the *Larousse Encyclopaedia of Music* — incredible when you consider the talent it has turned out, from the Howard Morrison Quartet on — and there is a similar story in other fields, with the Shakies being either left out or reduced to a footnote. That is the price chameleons pay. The emergence of Kiwese culture is changing all this and is making sure that people sit up, take notice and understand. Years ago Australians thought pop singer Johnny Devlin was in real estate because he said that back in New Zealand he had a lot of 'huts'. No one thinks that now of Crowded House; Kiwese has already made its mark.

The Kiwese Dictionary

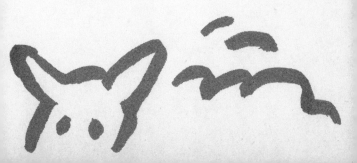

A

abrist Aware of, cognisant with: e.g. 'I want to be kipped abrist of all divilopments,' sid the department hid.

adjustment Place where livestock is boarded and cared for: 'I've got my kettle in adjustment' is what a farmer would say when the cattle are in agistment.

a medgen Visualise, conjure up mentally. John Lennon's first solo album *Imagine* was a 'bug hut' in NZ. Even today, the railway tunnels of Australian cities are filled with Kiwi buskers singing:

A medgen there's no countries
A brotherhood of men
A medgen all the people
Loving for today . . . you hoo . . . etc.

a nelly sus Methodical examination. There has
been very little analysis of the two Tasman
countries and their interaction. Most
commentators prefer to do an 'a nelly sus' of
Anglo-French relations, particularly those which
involve five-star restaurants.

Asteer Dancer 'Frid Asteer' was very popular in
NZ. For many years it was the done thing to
call out his name at the football whenever a
player sidestepped an opponent instead of
running into him and being tackled. Fred
Astaire's partners included 'Junja' Rogers, 'Ill in
her' Powell, and 'Sud' Charisse.

a ton of peers Not a delegation from the House
of Lords, but a metallic container full of fruit.
NZ gourmets always ask for 'Bartlett peers'.
Goulburn Valley and Ardmona are popular
brands throughout the Antipodes. Many Kiwis
find seasonal work picking pears at 'Ship a ton,
Vuctoria'.

Auckers Affectionate nickname for yacht-mad Auckland, the City of Sails. Unfortunately, American visitors pronounce it 'Ockers' which means, in Kiwese, 'Australians'.

Awake and Sung Condensed version of the Clifford Odets play *Awake and Sing*.

a weir Abreast with, cognisant of: e.g. 'I was not a weir that my phone was being tepped,' he complained.

B

Beckster James K. Baxter was one of New
  Zealand's leading poets.

beer 1. Endure, withstand. One Kiwese-speaker
  said he stopped frequenting the New Zealand
  Hotel in Sydney because of rising prices and
  changing clientele: 'I couldn't beer to go to the
  place again,' he said. Alas, the New Zealand
  Hotel is now the Australian Museum Hotel. 2.
  Furry mammal found in NZ zoos. 'Gruzzly
  beers' are *not* to be found roaming the mountains
  of the Shaky Isles; there are no animals native
  to NZ. 'Tiddy beers' are favourites with the

'cuds', who also love to see the 'koala beers' when they visit Oz. A Kiwi with a hangover could be described as 'a beer with a sore hid'.

Beethoven Elgar Rugby footballer. Beethoven and Elgar are popular composers in Kiwiland, along with Thomas 'Tell Us' and 'Wreck Mennen Off', but one of the first of the All Blacks was a player called Beethoven Algar (proof supplied on request).

bell kenny Not a firm of Irish solicitors, but a small veranda. Also used in theatre terminology ('Stalls, Driss Circle or Bell Kenny, sir?'). Not to be confused with Cull Kinny, as in the cliché 'fighting like a peer of Cull Kinny kets'. Some irreverent Australians have suggested that the NZ flag is a wet towel hanging over a 'bell kenny'.

Bess Name of strait north of Tasmania.

betch Weekender: e.g. 'Thet's a great betch, Bivan,' Sid Hither.

betting 'Betting gloves' are worn by 'betsmen' in 'crucket'.

Bex Sir Arnold 'Bex' is popular in New Zealand for his soothing melodies. In Oz, Bex is a headache powder, and a brand of German beer

— Beck's — which is popular among travelling Kiwis.

bicker Argumentative male tennis players have been lambasted in the New Zealand press, especially when they criticise local officials. Teutonic superstars Boris 'Bicker', Michael 'Stuck' and Alex 'Enter Nutch' are especially unwelcome. They do, however, get excited about 'Stiffy' Graf.

bint Crooked. Bent Street in Sydney is named after the former Judge-Advocate Ellis Bent, a friend of the Rev. Samuel Marsden.

Blear Surname, as in Jock 'Blear'. Playwright Ron 'Blear' is the author of *The Crustean Brothers*.

bledder Part of human anatomy. Specifically, a sack for 'pus'. Those who suffer prostate trouble and take a long time to void the bladder may be asked by a Kiwi doctor, 'Uz your Bledisloe?'

Blunt's New York sandwich. At Sarnie's Takeaway in Auckland you can get all kinds of ethnic

food. Remember, ethnic Enzedders have been assimilated, so if you want a blintz ask for a 'Blunt's'.

Blustering Force which chafes and raises welts. Also used metaphorically, as in 'Thet was a blustering drive by Mark Greatbetch.'

Bread Popular boy's name. Tennis player 'Bread' Gilbert is a drawcard in New Zealand.

brickfast Heavy, quick meal in early morning. Popular dishes include 'sheep's lover' (lamb's fry), 'fruit cellared' (fruit salad) and 'Igs Bin a Duct' (Eggs Benedict).

brist Part of human anatomy between 'nick' and 'billy'. New Zealanders tend to get their classical quotes right and will say, 'Musuc hath charms to soothe the sevage brist.' Australians, on the other hand, are more slapdash with inherited clichés and will most likely say, 'Music hath charms to soothe the savage beast', and take it to mean you can enter a lion's cage playing the flute. In NZ the female 'brists' are venerated, as they are in England, where they are known by the slightly longer 'Bristols' (Bristol City = titty).

Britt A girl's name in Scandinavia, but a boy's
name in Kiwese. 'Britt' Steven is a leading NZ
'tinnus' player.

'brung a plate' Throughout Australasia it is
common to Bring Your Own Grog or Bring a
Plate to a party. If Kiwis say 'brung a plate'
they are not referring to a previous occasion, they
are talking about the future.

brusque trading Speedy exchange of goods for
money; high turnover.

Bucks Money was not the goal of cornet player
Bix Beiderbecke, who died in poverty. For NZ
jazz fans, there is a place in the heart for the
man they simply called 'Bucks'.

buds fear Old-fashioned journalese expression
meaning 'has a chance': e.g. 'Otago buds fear
towards becoming the Ruviera of the South
Pacufuc.' Also, part of tendering process: e.g.

'The job of the Ombudsmen uz to insure thet for government tinders all the buds are fear'.

buff Tactic used to distract opponents in football. Will Auckland turn on the 'buff'? A staple tabloid headline in Australia is 'Saints to turn on biff.' When Kiwi coach Graham Lowe was at 'Maori–Warringah' he said, 'We're not going to feature in the buff.'

bugger In Australia this means, strictly speaking, sheep-shagger. The speaker of Kiwese, however, knows that across the Tasman 'bugger' means larger, as in 'Mine's bugger then yours' or 'The bugger they are, the harder they fall.'

bug hut Not a de-lousing station nor anything like it. This means 'lusty blow', as in 'Thet's a bug hut. It sucks! The ball's landed on the top dick of the Mimber's Stend!'

built up The Road Safety Council has exhorted people in many languages to fasten their seat belts. In Kiwese-speaking areas people were urged to 'Built up!'

bulge Unwanted ballast. Sea water that has seeped into the hold.

bulk To cheat, to gyp, to con. Phil Silvers played the aptly named Sergeant Bilko in a popular television series. This character was adept at bilking his colleagues out of their hard-earned cash. In more recent times the collapse of the John Valentine Health Studios left many people 'bulked'.

bun button To have inflicted on one an unsolicited carnivorous overture: e.g. 'I've bun button by a mosquito! Pass the Rud.' Any Kiwi visitor to Oz who has 'bun button' by a spider or snake should seek professional help.

bundy eyes In New South Wales, visiting Kiwis soon learn about bindiis, the prickly plant too often found underfoot. They pronounce this 'bundy eyes', but should note that in some parts of Queensland 'Bundy eyes' means inebriated, as Bundaberg Rum is very popular.

Bung 'Bung' Lee is a retailer of electrical appliances. 'I bought the vudeo at Bung's' is a standard defence in some Kiwi circles.

bunt Old-fashioned term for sheila (in Arabic, bint = daughter.)

busk Seafood bisque is popular with fish-mad Kiwis. They pronounce it 'busk', which in Oz means to sing for money in the street. Paradoxically, most buskers in Oz are from New Zealand, and can be seen rendering the greatest hits of Bill and Boyd in shopping malls from Rockhampton to Manjimup.

butt A piece of ass in the US, but just a piece in Kiwese. A 'butt' of trouble in NZ can be anything from a riot to a stalled Vauxhall. 'She took the butt between her teeth,' said a Kiwi commentator of an athlete.

butter Tart. Not sweet. The most famous brand in this line is Angostura Bitters. 'They've been married so long they're on their sickened bottle of Engostura Butters' — old Kiwi saying.

buzness Business. In many cases Kiwese is more logical than normal English. Business *should* be pronounced 'buzness', judging by the spelling, and that's just what New Zealanders do. It was a pity that George Bernard Shaw, who advocated aligning spelling and pronunciation, was not acquainted with the joys of Kiwese.

C

cheer A welcome piece of furniture for those with tired legs. Often found beside tables. NZ-born New South Wales Premier John Fahey said he 'cheered' the committee which made Sydney's Olympic 'bud'.

cheery Full of *bonhomie* and *joie de vivre* in Australia, but in Kiwese this word has the opposite meaning — usually fearful, suspicious, apprehensive. Many linguists have been chary about saying Kiwis pronounce chary 'cheery', but that is mainly because they are leery.

chick out 'Chick-out chucks' in supermarkets
prefer to be called point-of-sale operators. Many
of these girls are Kiwese-speakers called Heather
or Jackie or Rhonda and they work at 'Cheddar'
(Chadstone Shopping Centre) or the credit-
driven 'Rose Lends'.

chully bun An Esky.

chunk 1. Piece, bit, small shaft, opening: e.g. A
chunk of light showed under the door. 2. (derog.)
Resident or expatriate of or from large oriental
nation: e.g. 'I wouldn't eat chopped shark tail
— that's Chunk food.'

chunned her In some Australian east coast
drinking circles, to swallow something is to
'neck it': e.g. 'He gave me a double daiquiri and
I necked it.' The opposite of this is to 'chin
her', meaning to vomit, to wear your stomach
on your chin: e.g. 'I had a double daiquiri but
five minutes later I chinned her.' In Kiwese this
last bit is pronounced 'chunned her' and is
believed to be the origin of the expression
'chunder'.

Clear Kiwis are much more precise than Sydneysiders. There is no muddying of the waters as far
as ancestry is concerned. In Sydney it is not
the done thing to ask any questions, possibly

because of the city's convict origins, but there are
no such constraints where people from En Zed
are concerned. I once asked a girl from the
Shakies where her forebears had come from.
'Ireland,' she said promptly, 'County Clear.'

cluck Noise made by unloaded gun. Also,
expression meaning sympatico, as in, 'We
clucked.' Sometimes computer dating couples
don't get on, they just don't 'cluck'. Others are
happier, and you hear them say, 'We eventually
clucked.' More passionate Kiwis confess that
they 'clucked' on the first date.

clucky Disposed towards cronyism, prone to
associating with a clique. Cricketers are supposed
to be 'clucky', as are former espionage agents.
In Oz, 'clucky' means anticipating motherhood
or hearing the biological clock. Some women in
their thirties are said to be 'on the last train
to Clucksville'. The term comes from the
onomatopoeic sound of a mother hen.

Clumped Surname of Austrian artist. Gustav Klimt is a hit in Australia, too.

clunk Noise made by closing door, especially in jail. Slang term for gaol itself: e.g. 'I dudn't have an Ella buy, so the boys un blue threw me un the clunk.'

colour Terminator, violent forecloser of human life. Several NZ films have dealt with 'mess colours'. The increasing availability of guns is blamed for this rise in the number of 'colours on the loose'. In an anti-smoking campaign in the Shakies, cigarettes were described as 'lady colours'.

Come Novel by Rudyard Kipling which has long been a standard text in NZ. It is not pornographic, although it is set in 'Undia'.

Come Kemble Canada's first woman Prime Minister.

Come Youse Controversial captain of Oz cricket team who resigned tearfully in favour of Allan Border. 'Come' had insisted that all deliveries be overarm. Full name: Kimberley John Hughes.

Conned Luff and Eerie Not a three-partner law firm, but a pair of historians. There are many excellent books on the Shaky Isles, such as

A Short History of New Zealand, by J.B. Condliffe and W.T.G. Airey.

construction Tight, choking effect. This is the effect construction sites have on traffic in Australia, but for a Kiwi a 'construction' is an impediment, a blockage, a 'restruction'.

Coupling Non-pornographic Commonwealth author who wrote *Kim* and *The Jungle Book*. First name: Rudyard. One of 'Coupling's' most famous characters, Mrs Bathurst, came from Auckland.

Crekhov Not a Russian playwright, but rather the start of, or signal for, or sound made by. Two Kiwi colloquialisms are 'fear crekhov the whup' (give me a fair go) and 'the crekhov dawn wouldn't be safe . . .' (he is a randy person).

Crosby, Stulls end Nesh Pop group that once boasted Neil Young. Ray Martin revealed on 'A Current, A Fear' that a Kiwi who had just spent four years in Oz answered 'Crosby, Steels

and Nash' on a quiz show and lost, according
to the judges. The man actually said 'Stills' but,
just as Sydney sounds like 'Seedney' to the New
Zealand ear, so he was wrong for failing to say
'Stulls'. The decision was overturned on appeal.

crucket NZ cricket has produced many interesting
characters such as 'Blear' Pocock, Mark
'Greatbetch' and Richard 'Headley'. The most
successful captains have been 'Bivan' Congdon,
'Jiff' Howarth and 'Jirra me' Coney. All-
rounder Bob Cunis was criticised by the English
press for having a name that was neither one
thing nor the other. Less equivocal have been the
'Dux' — 'Duck' Motz, Art 'Duck', 'Duck' de
Groen. The most famous ground in NZ is the
glamorously named Basin Reserve in
'Willington'. Many Kiwis have a vast knowledge
of Australian cricket — although they tend
to mix up Sam Trimble and Hugh Trumble —
but the reverse cannot be said; many Australians
are indifferent to the triumphs of New Zealand
cricket, and tend to mix up George Headley
and Richard Hadlee.

crumb Breaker of the law. Parking fine evaders
— of whom a high proportion are Kiwis — are
locked up in Sydney gaols with 'hardened

crumbs'. Several of these crims have protested at
the injustice of such a system.

Crump 1. Surname of Barry Crump, distinguished
NZ writer, formerly married to poet Fleur
Adcock. 2. Styling of hair, particularly curling
or waving it. 3. Handicap or hinder.

crux Injuries to the neck, usually caused by jolting
or sudden movement: e.g. The bus stopped
suddenly and the pessengers suffered crux in their
nix.

cud Young goat. Also young human being, child.
In the early days of TV a great favourite with
viewers was *The Susco Cud*. In the early days of
NZ, when cannibalism was acceptable in the
South Pacific, the expression 'chewing on your
cud' took on realistic overtones.

cult Item of clothing worn by obsessive minority.
The 'cult' is a Scottish pleated tartan skirt made
from wool. It is worn by both sexes, the 'leds'
and the 'lessees'.

Cumberland Kimba the White Lion was a popular children's television character who lived in Kimbaland. For Kiwese-speaking children this was 'Cumberland'.

cuppa A breakfast favourite, especially with Anglophiles. A small fish that has been cleaned and smoked.

cuss 'You must rimimber thus, a cuss is just a cuss . . .' Do New Zealanders 'cuss' a lot? The answer to this is 'Yiss!'

cussin' cousins In the 1890s, as the six Australian colonies moved towards Federation, New Zealand was offered 'a seat on the board'. They rejected the offer to amalgamate for fear of being swamped by Aussies. Besides, alleges historian Keith Sinclair, they 'felt superior' to Australians. The grounds for this superiority are not clear, but the kissing cousins fell out for some years before being brought together by television.

cut Equipment, especially for sport: e.g. 1. 'I made the cut,' said Mr Slazenger. 2. 'Dud you bring the cut?' Sid the scupper. The plural is 'cuts'. Note: Modern-day teaching kits have nothing to do with the old-fashioned 'cuts', which was an overt form of punishment.

D

das lick–suck It may sound like a service
provided by German sex workers, but it
means predisposed towards transposition of
letters and words. Eg. 'dias' for 'dais'. Note:
David Lange was *not* being dyslexic when he
called Fall-Out Out-Fall. The big man did not
approve of the portrayal of him in this television
drama.

day old chuck Young poultry, not dried
vomit.

Deafness end Chloe Music suite by Maurice
Ravel, more cheerful than it sounds.

Dear Much-loved cartoon character, the intrepid pilot Dan Dare, is affectionately called Dan 'Dear' in New Zealand.

dearie A place where milk products are made. NZ is famous for its ice cream and other high quality 'dearie' exports. Blossom Dearie has toured New Zealand successfully, but only after overcoming misconceptions that she was a brand name, not a singer.

Deli Short for Dalmatian. Traditionally, New Zealand has favoured immigrants from the British Isles and Holland. They did let in about 101 Dalmatians, however, and then in the 1980s it became fashionable to reveal part-Maori ancestry.

dense Movement of the body to music. 'Modern dense' was made popular in NZ through the films of Fred 'Asteer' and 'Junja' Rogers.

Derryn Boy's name. Spelt and pronounced 'Darren' in most parts of the English-speaking world.

difference Respect for, obedience to: e.g. 'Un difference to her peer runts' wushes, N.R. Peck One dud not see the R-rated *The Pee Enno*.'

dill legation A group of persons representing the government at a conference. New Zealand sent a large delegation to the first United Nations conference in 1945 and has been active in 'geo polla-tucks' ever since.

dimmer kretz Those who believe in democracy.

din Home of the brave lion. Generations of Kiwi children have heard the story of Daniel and the Lion's 'Din'.

Dinchas In Oz, 'Dincha' is a contraction of 'Didn't you?' 'Dinchas', by extension, means 'Didn't youse?' In Kiwese, however, 'dinchas' are false teeth.

'dirryn, I love you!' 'In Zid' superstar Derryn Hinch has many fans, especially Kiwi women, who mob him and shout endearments.

disparate Desperate. Some observers felt it was desperate to be disparate in Auckland in the 1950s.

dith end Texas Mark Twain said the inevitable things in life were death and taxes. This is only half true for the inhabitants of Australia's

Kiwese Homelands areas, who insist on being paid in cash for services rendered. The goods and services tax was designed to raise revenue from this black economy but, in an ironic twist, the GST was imposed in New Zealand but not Australia. Kiwis in Australia have traditionally been reluctant to pay their 'Texas' on income earned, but with the rejection of the GST by the electorate, they will not even have to pay taxes on goods they buy. To be fair, the idea of an expatriate community living off the black economy was pioneered by Australians living in London's Earls Court.

dome onion New Zealand became a 'dome onion' in 1907, although it retained many traditional 'lunks' with the UK. Today, the leading newspaper in Wellington is *The Dominion*. It, too, is self-governing.

done Loud noise. 'Stop that din!' Bondi residents once shouted at renting Kiwis. Settled En Zedders are now heard shouting 'Stop thet done!' at newer arrivals.

Double James Dibble was an ABC newsreader whose style was copied by many Kiwi immigrants, people who called him 'James Double' when they arrived. Dibble spoke

standard Australian English, and many of
his acolytes tried to turn themselves into a
carbon copy of 'Muster Double'. Channel Nine
in Sydney has had only two main newsreaders
in its history — Brian Henderson and David
Low. As is the case with other diligent former
Kiwis like Harry M. Miller, Dennis Grant, Jane
Campion, Frank Devine, Cathy Downs and
Colin Segelov, no one knows they are former
Kiwis. The only giveaway is when they say
'Seedney'.

double dutch Twin trenches, usually dug around
camping sites by extra-keen campers.

Doubly Tennis player Colin Dibley was described
by an NZ commentator as 'bug-serving Col
Doubly'.

dovey To 'dovey' up the spoils means to share the
proceeds.

drunks Do not be alarmed if a Kiwi hostess invites
you around for 'drunks'.

duck-hid Term of abuse directed at men.
LOMBARD was an acronym popular in Sydney's
eastern suburbs. It stands for 'Lots Of Money
But A Real Dick-head'.

duck lover Cat food. Also, a nymphomaniac.
Note: In some circles duck liver is eaten by
humans. In some circles a dick lover is just a
healthy red-blooded woman. In some circles a
duck lover is an animal liberationist.

Duck Quacks It sounds like a truism, but it
is the name of one of New Zealand's finest
runners. Dick Quax won many medals for his
country as a middle-distance star of the
seventies.

Dudley Surname of American rhythm 'n' blues
singer. The Bo Diddley beat was a big influence
on rock bands of the sixties in the Shaky Isles.

dud time In Oz, to say you had a 'dud time'
means you did not enjoy yourself. In Kiwese, to
say 'I dud time' means you are an ex-convict.

duff Part of a car. When your differential is in a
terminal stage a Kiwi mechanic will tell you
straight out, 'You've stuffed your duff.' In Oz the
term indicates a state of impregnation, with a
causal link to 'stuffing'.

duffer Dull clichés are not unknown in Kiwese, with such favourites as 'We agreed to duffer', 'I big to duffer' and 'Duffer rent strokes for duffer rent folks' leading the way.

duff thongs More than a vowel, the diphthong differs in Kiwese. Bare is pronounced 'beer', a fact recognised by the Auckland shop 'Beer Essentials', which adorns Queen Street. In Australia, 'duff thongs' are sandals with soft soles used for stealing cattle (rare).

Duffy cult 1. Not easy. 2. Admirers of former Attorney-General Michael Duffy. 3. Title of newsletter about doings of former Brisbane footballer Shane Duffy. 4. Skirt worn by Duffy clan.

dull Uninspiring cucumber-like vegetable or herb.

dumb Not bright: e.g. The lights of New Plummeth are dumb in the must.

Dumb Pull Brand of whisky sold in a distinctive
bottle with three dimples. 'Dumb Pull whusky'
is 'fufteen' years old.

dung Sound made by gong. Also means punch,
as in 'Uf you don't built up, I'll dung you.'

Dunnesty US television soap opera starred Joan
Collins as 'Elixirs Kerrungton'.

Dunny Pails Tennis coach and former Davis Cup
star Dinny Pails joined Jack Kramer's travelling
professional troupe along with fellow
countryman 'Kin' McGregor. According to
legend, in an Auckland hotel he was paged thus:
'Muster Dunny Pails!' and several alarmed
tourists had to be reassured that yes, NZ *did*
have a sewerage system.

dutch doug Trench excavated: e.g. 'I want that
dutch doug,' said the foreman, pointing to the
picks and shovels. Not to be confused with
Aussie Bob. Note: the cliché 'as dull as dutch
water' can be sometimes heard used by Kiwese
speakers. It is not intended as any sort of
comment on the heroic struggle of the people of
The Netherlands to keep the sea at bay.

'Dutch the monarchy!' Many older Kiwis are
alarmed by Australia's republican plans to ditch
the Royal Family. Republicanism is not as

strong a movement in New Zealand, which was
once known as 'Ungland's most dutiful
daughter'. In England, of course, to 'dutch the
monarchy' would involve bringing over from
Holland one of the descendants of William of
Orange.

E

ear Mixture of nitrogen and oxygen. There is no
need to be alarmed if a Kiwi invites you to an
'open ear' performance of *Hamlet*; only the King
gets poisoned through the ear. It simply means
that the play will be performed alfresco. An
invitation to an 'open ear luncheon' simply means
that you will be eating out of doors, depending
on the 'wither'.

ear roebucks Cardio-vascular exercise class at
the 'jum'.

Ear's Rock Now called Uluru, this attracted many
Kiwi shutterbugs, and still does. Other tourist

landmarks they favour include 'the Cumberleys', 'the Pulbara' and 'the Ellis'.

East Lunn Popular 'miller' drama, often performed at NZ's many 'dunner' theatres.

Ebbet wars Slaughtering house for 'kettle'. The sight of cattle grazing near the abattoirs on the outskirts of Auckland can be a grim one, although at least the condemned are eating a hearty meal — the grass is a deep green.

Ecks Brand of soft drink in Oz; sharp tool in NZ.

effect A truthful, unchallengeable piece of information. Flamboyant lawyers often begin sentences with this rhetorical flourish: 'Uz ut effect that you . . .?' Also used colloquially, as in 'I've head enough and thet's effect.'

ekka dymocks University staff. Most English lecturers have bravely denied the existence of Kiwese — even NZ academics, who call themselves 'In Zid ekka dymocks'. Note: In Oz the phrase 'Ekka Dymocks' would mean 'bookstore at the Brisbane Exhibition'.

elementary To do with basic nutrition. The 'elementary' canal is the part of the human anatomy where food is processed.

Elf Man's name, short for Alfred.

el frisco In the 'open ear', out of doors, under the stars.

Ella buy Legal term meaning proof of whereabouts. If you were somewhere else when a video was stolen, then you have an 'Ella buy'. Some Kiwi visitors may have been confused by a headline which read ELLA BUY: SAINTS DENY. This simply referred to a bid to sign up footballer Mark Ella and had nothing to do with any alibi.

Ella Gee Film star June Allyson (*'The Glyn Muller Story'*) graced many quality productions. Her real name was Ella Geisman and this talented, unaffected actress was simply 'Ella G' to friends. In Kiwese, however, Ella Gee is not a person but an aversion to a particular substance or season. People with an 'Ella Gee' to cats usually start sneezing as soon as they enter a room where a 'ket' has been. In Oz it means lament, as in the sad poem 'Ella Gee in a Country Churchyard'.

Ellen Elder Star of TV series 'Mesh'.

Ellis a first name for girls in Kiwese — as in *'Ellis un Wonderlend'* — but a surname in Oz — as in 'Artist Bob Ellis drew gasps.'

Ends Us Three-way defence alliance involving Australia, New Zealand and the US. The 'Ends Us' Pact was signed in the aftermath of the declaration of war in Korea. The first meeting of the ANZUS Council took place in Honolulu in 1952. In 1984 the election of David Lange as Prime Minister of New Zealand shook the Pact to its foundations. He banned US nuclear ships on the basis that it would only take 'one explosion and that ends us'. Diplomatic relations between Washington and Wellington have not fully recovered, and the ANZUS Pact is in 'lumbo'.

Engels 'A game of Engels' was Onny Parun's description of tennis. This did not mean that a country club sport had been taken over by radicals. Snooker is another 'game of Engels', as is, to a lesser extent, billiards. Those who have mastered these angles and represented New Zealand at tennis include, apart from Parun,

'Frenk Renouf', 'Cruss Lewis', 'Killy Ivendin' and
'Brian Fearley'.

Errol Dighton Not, as seems likely, an English
'B' movie actor of the fifties, but a phrase
indicating positive healing action. If something
breaks — like a vase — the practical Kiwi will
put some Araldite on it. This comes out as 'Put
some Errol Dighton ut.'

Error buck Language spoken in countries like
'Surria', 'E. Jupp' and 'The Libber Non', as well
as in the kitchens of some of NZ's best
restaurants. Many Arabic speakers come from
merchant stock and, paradoxically, make few
errors with their bucks.

error route Arnott's famous oval-shaped biscuits
are available in the Shakies, where they are
known, in Kiwese, as 'mulk error route buskets'.

Ethel A girl's name in Oz, but a guy's name in
Kiwese. The Seekers have a bass player called

Athol Guy. Kiwi hoboes have been evicted from 'Ethel Wharf' in Sydney.

ever cadeau Fruit/vegetable called Avo's in Oz greengrocers' shops where apostrophes are used to keep the food fresh.

Ex-Munster Kind of carpet. In Oz, the term either means 'Out of Ireland' or it refers to an actor's credits: e.g. Fred Gwynne was an ex-Munster.

F

fear Pale, pallid, blond. 'Fear hear' is seen as
   desirable by some Kiwis and is usually achieved
   with the aid of peroxide. A 'fear complixion', or
   looking as white as a sheet, is also sought
   after in some quarters.

fears Monies owing for cost of journey. Kiwi bus
   conductors used to be heard calling out 'Fears
   please' all over Sydney.

Feral Irish surname. Oxymoronic racing man 'Pet
   Feral' was a Kiwi and, like many of his
   countrymen, wrote for the *Daily Mirror* in
   Sydney. A good judge of horseflesh, as befits his

place of origin, Pat Farrell was well respected by Oz punters. Not so well received was President Manuel Farrell of Argentina. When Argentina sought admission to the United Nations, New Zealand's Prime Minister, Peter Fraser, was critical of the wild and way-out regime of the man he called 'Muster Feral'.

Fibbery Deceptively cold second month of the year. Some spoilt Australians claim that the Kiwis are good at football because, as it is a winter game, they can play it for ten months of the year. It is certainly true that cricketers in NZ feel overshadowed by the almighty 'All Blex', but it would be wrong to suggest that this is because the cricket season only lasts a few weeks. Just the same, the Australian visitor should take an overcoat, even for a trip in 'Fibbery' because, as the locals confess, the next stop is Antarctica.

fight fear NZ footballers are traditionally exhorted to 'fight fear', as the country's supremacy in the sport has been built on tenacity and aggression. To 'fight fear' you use your 'fust' on an opponent rather than 'kuck' him. When Richard Loe used his 'ilbow' on Australian player Paul Carozza, occasioning grievous

bodily harm, he was stoutly defended by his
fellow countrymen. It was only later that Loe was
suspended for using his 'fungus' on an
opponent's eyeball.

fitter Cheney A kind of pasta. It was misleading
to Kiwese speakers when Lithgow boxer Spike
Cheney went on a diet and forswore fettucine.
The commentators talked about a 'fitter
Cheney'. Pasta lovers who visit Kiwese
Homelands restaurants in Australia should also
note that rigatoni comes out as 'Rugger Tony'
and tagliatelle as 'Tell ya, Tilly'.

Five Bills Poem by Kenneth Slessor (not his real
name) about the drowning of Kiwi sculptor Joe
'Lunch', who was believed to be in debt at the
time. A talented cartoonist, 'Lunch' fell off a
Sydney Harbour ferry wearing a raincoat with
bottles of beer stuffed in the pockets. 'Five Bills'
is a memorial to the artist, an Ella Gee.

flea-ear Bright light used as a signal. A flare path is a series of such lights. 'Fire a flea-ear!' is a command sometimes heard on board an NZ Navy 'frugget'.

floppy dusk There is little twilight in New Zealand; night just falls. Visitors from the northern hemisphere often miss the long evenings of their summer.

fluck The sack, the bullet, being fired. Also, real name of English film star Diana Dors (née Diane Fluck). In Oz there are many expressions for being given the flick — the four o'clock shove, being awarded the DCM (Don't Come Monday) and being told 'It's a nice day for travelling', not to mention the euphemisms such as Downsizing, Rationalisation and Reallocation of Human Resources. In Kiwese it is simply a matter of being 'govern the fluck'.

follow the just Understand the essentials, comprehend the kernel: e.g. 'I wasn't abrist of all the details of what was Sid, but I followed the just of ut.'

frenja penny Not a rare coin, but a tropical tree with flowers. If a Maori girl wears a frangipani flower behind her left ear, it usually means she looks even more 'fitchung'.

fuckle Capricious, lacking constancy: e.g. 'The audiences are fuckle', said the director of Auckland's Mercury Theatre after a losing season, 'What would they know? Fuckle!'

'Fuddler on the Roof' In Australia it was a 'hut' with New Zealanders, but not so when it toured the Shakies. Who can figure it?

fuggers Numerals. Having a 'hid for fuggers' usually means a career as a chartered accountant. Also means silhouettes, as in 'fuggers un a lendscape' or character, as in 'He made a duck and lift the ground a dijicted fugger.' Figures can also appear in clichés such as 'Thet fuggers' or 'See uf you Ken fugger thus out.'

fulm The New Zealand 'fulm undustry' has made a tremendous 'um pecked' since it got going in the 1980s. Jane Campion, Russell Crowe and Roger Donaldson are three of the big names thrown up, although radio personality Pam

Corkery introduced a sobering note when she said she 'dudn't like *The Pee Enno*'.

'Fulthy Futz!' All Black 'scupper' Sean Fitzpatrick was excoriated after biting the ear of a South African and vice versa.

fun Shark fun soup is a speciality with NZ's Chinese community. Do the Chinese, Maoris and Uzbekistanis in the Shakies say 'fungus' instead of fingers? Yiss!

Funland Dour sub-arctic country in northern Europe which has sent forth immigrants to (comparatively) sunny New Zealand. The capital of 'Funland' is 'Hill Sunkey'.

Funny English actor. 'L. Bert Funny' starred in 'Ennie'.

fush Marine creature. The tattooed fisherman in briny runners reeling in a sweep from a rock on the South Coast of New South Wales will in 90 cases out of a hundred be a Kiwi.

fux Whenever someone rigs a fight or a football match it is called a 'fux' in Kiwese. Also means predicament, as in the dialogue cliché, 'Thus uz a fine fux you've got us unto.' In Oz the equivalent expression is 'stew'.

fuzz Effervescent effect. A 'fuzzy drunk' is a carbonated soft drink, not a hallucinating lush.

American visitors might think that 'fuzz' is something to do with the police, or that a drink with some 'fuzz' in it is laced, like a 'Muckey Fun', with a knock-out drop. In fact, the only strong drink in this line is the gin fizz.

fuzz id Physical education. En Zed schools are attractive and spacious and well planned. It is a common sight to see school students doing 'Fuzz Id' classes on the playing-fields as you drive past.

G

glummer Are Kiwis dour and pessimistic? Do they lack the cheerful brashness of the Oz? A 'glummer of hope' is in fact an optimistic phrase. There is no evidence that New Zealanders are glummer than Australians. In Kiwese 'glummer' also means a flicker or a twinkle or a glow of light.

glunt Sexually-overtoned saying among older Kiwis begins, 'Win I was just a glunt in my father's eye . . .' Another meaning of 'glunting' is flashing.

Glyn Lovett Brand of whisky.

〉〉

govern Vouchsafed, granted, transferred free of
charge. Speaking of a great opera star, one Kiwi
said, 'Curry te Kenawa has God-govern gufts.'
The film '*Unforgovern*' starred 'Clunt' Eastwood.
In some remote Homelands cinemas tickets
had to be 'govern' away.

Greville Stones used in mixing concrete.

Grummett NZ cricketer Clarrie Grimmett
migrated to Australia from Dunedin in 1914
when he was in his twenties. Nicknamed 'Grum'
because of his grim face and Kiwi accent,
Grimmett finally won selection to play for
Australia in 1925. He held his place until 1936,
when he retired from Test cricket at the age
of 45. So fond was he of the baggy green
cap of his adopted country that he wore it at
all times, even when bowling. The wizened,
respected Grimmett should not be confused with
the Oz term 'grommett', which means young
surfer.

guess Flammable vapour used in stoves. In the
earth's atmosphere oxygen is the second 'guess'
to nitrogen.

Guffawed 1. Laughed heartily. 2. Surname, as
English cricketer Norman Gifford discovered.

gulls Where there are fish, there are 'gulls', which are found at the side of the marine creatures and are used for breathing underwater.

gut Term of abuse, as in 'Pompous gut!' Media critic Stuart Littlemore has upset some sections of the media, who have retaliated by criticising Littlemore. One of their descriptions of him, 'Pompous git', floats past in the credits of the show. In Kiwese, a randy 'gut' is a highly 'sixed' person, while a Scouse 'gut' is an immigrant from Liverpool. A beer 'gut' is a tardy waiter in a lounge bar, while 'lots of guts' means a large number of incompetent and foolish persons.

Hell Burg That's what they called Sydney during the great bush fires of 1994. In Kiwese, however, it is the name of one of their greatest athletes, Murray Halberg, whose fans used to chant 'Hell Burg! Hell Burg!' when he won a race.

here Growth on human scalp. Also, species of large rabbit. The cross-country running game, 'Here and Hounds' has fallen in popularity in recent years. The casserole dish 'jugged here' is also less popular.

Herod's A store in London.

hex Are New Zealand newspapers cursed with 'hex'? A hack is an undistinguished writer, a literary jobsworth. On most NZ newspapers and journals you will find the usual mixture of thoroughbreds and hacks. Academia is not immune to the curse of the 'hex'. One Kiwi author told me that the *History of Whackatinya* (not its real name) was written by a 'team of hex'. Some parts of '*The Lustner*', a weekly magazine, are extremely well written, while other parts are clearly the work of hacks. Many distinguished Kiwi journalists — Susan Chenery, Frank Harris, Shona Martyn, Spiro Zavos — have emigrated to Australia, and some of their places have been taken by 'hex'.

hick Exclamation, euphemism for hell: e.g. 'What the hick . . .?', 'You've got a hick of a nerve . . .'

Hicked American writer Ben Hecht was once described on NZ radio as 'Bin Hicked'. He was the co-author of the play *The Front Page* which was revived in the Shakies because it had been revived in the UK. Hecht and his long-time collaborator Charles Macarthur did not regard themselves as writers with a high degree of literary prestige. They cheerfully acknowledged that they were 'hex'.

hid Top part of human anatomy, the cranium, the
north island, the melon, the noggin. To answer
the question, 'Where are a footballer's brains?'
in Kiwese you should say, 'Their hid.' Do not
say, or mean, 'They're hid.'

hill-raisers Film stars, mainly of Celtic origin,
who drink and shout in public places. Errol
Flynn, Peter O'Toole, Oliver Reed and Mickey
Rourke were typical, along with 'The Richards
of the Earth' — Burton, Harris, Johnson etc.
Kiwi stars Bruno Lawrence and Sam Neill are
not hell-raisers. Indeed, with NZ actors
generally it is a sorry story of pipe-smoking,
ethnic wives, art gallery openings and university
degrees.

hinchmen Cronies, off-siders, side-kicks, mates,
followers. Not to be confused with the staff of
television personality 'Dirryn Hunch', who was
born in the Shakies. Gangsters have henchmen,

but television personalities have staffers and
gophers.

Hindo Durable Channel Nine star Brian
Henderson is known as 'Hendo' to his Australian
friends, and 'Hindo' to his fellow Kiwis.

'How's trucks?' Ungrammatical but widely used
greeting among lorry drivers in New Zealand
and, by extension, Bondi and other Kiwese
Homelands in Australia.

Hugs The warm regard in which Ray Higgs is
held in Kiwi circles can be explained by this
overheard remark: 'He plays football like a New
Zealander.'

hull, Hullary Mountain, mountain climber. It is
typical of the contrast between the hyper
Australian and the understated Kiwi that what
is a mountain to the former is just a hill (or
'hull') to the latter. Sir Edmund Hillary
embodied this laconic spirit when he returned to
base camp after climbing Everest. 'We knocked
the bastard over,' he said.

Hullman Not a mountain climber, but a car. The
Hillman was a popular, if austere, brand of
British car, particularly the 'Hullman Monks'.
Other popular British cars in New Zealand were
the 'Armstrong-Sudley', the 'Jeguar' and the

popular, compact, economical 'Money'. Leyland
also brought out a successful 'Money', but they
failed with the much larger 'P70 Sucks'. Top of
the market, more expensive than the Rolls-
Royce, reputedly great for picking up girls, was
the 'Bintley'.

hunt Elusive trace, subtle suggestion: e.g. There
was a hunt of irony in the guide book's
discruption of Auckland as the Sparta of the
North. If a Kiwi says, 'Can't you take the hunt?'
it does not mean you are opposed to blood
sports.

Hutt man There is little Mafia activity in New
Zealand, although this is changing. For the time
being, a 'Hutt man' is not an assassin, but
simply a man from the Hutt Valley near
Wellington. Note: The Hutt Valley was *not*
once the Hutt Mountains. That comes from an
Australian joke about earthquakes. En Zedders
used not to be keen on jokes about their

seismic or linguistic heritage, but this is changing. They even make up jokes about themselves — mainly to do with sheep, of course — on all aspects of this thriving and mature society.

Hutton run Form of cricket in which the batsman must run if he hits the ball. *Not* invented by cricket legend 'Lynn' Hutton, who was definitely not the hit-and-run type.

I

Iccles bun Pastry, cake. 'He dud huz bun' = He
lost his temper.

Idi Popular boy's first name: e.g. Idi Barlow (SA)
scored a double sin cherie in the fourth Tist =
Eddie Barlow (South Africa) scored a double
century in the 4th Test. Short for Edward.

Ikea Common phrase in songs: e.g. 'Why should
Ikea?' and in dialogue: e.g. 'Of course Ikea.'
Not to be confused with the furniture store
IKEA.

ilk Same kind of animal as a moose or antelope.
Bulldogging 'ilks' from a 'hilicopter' is one of

NZ's more esoteric sports. Scottish aristocrat Sir
Iain Moncrieffe Of That Ilk never visited New
Zealand. Presumably, the portly Caledonian
was afraid of being addressed as 'Sir Iain
Moncrieffe of Thet 'Ulk'.

Il Sud An old film. 'Frenk Thrung was un Il Sud'
= Frank Thring was in *El Cid*.

Imbralla Now-defunct NSW country town. Once
as busy as a bee-hive, this mining centre was a
sister city to nearby Uralla and boasted 36
hotels in the main street alone. Because of the
heavy dew common at such an altitude, the
locals perfected a mobile shelter on a stick, one
of many uncredited Australian inventions (like
the ballot-box, the starting gate, and overarm
freestyle swimming). As is usually the case, most
of the miners in Imbralla were Kiwis, and when
they returned to NZ after the gold rush their
compatriots were most impressed by their wet
weather apparatus. 'Where dud you get thet?'
they asked. Thus was born the umbrella.
(Source: *Tall Tales Two*, by Perce P. Cassidy)

injun Machinery which causes motion in vehicle.
A 'two-stroke injun' does *not* refer to dour
Bombay batsman Dillip 'Dull' Vengsarkar.

inner me In Oz the 'inner me' is the soul, the
spirit or somesuch, but in the more paranoiac
outreaches of the Shaky Isles the 'inner me' is the
enemy.

J

Jeffrey's Store in Queen Street, Auckland; it is
spelt Jaffrey's. If it had been spelt Jeffrey's it
would have been pronounced 'Jiffrey's'. If it had
been spelt Jiffrey's it would have been
pronounced 'Juffrey's'. Who says New Zealand
vowels aren't round? They go in circles.

jendles Sandals, thongs, open shoes, jandals. In
En Zed the wearing of clog-like wooden warrior
sandals is common. In Australian beach-side
suburbs, however, a different message is sent out
by the average person wearing simple rubber
thongs. The message is, 'I am not going to kick

you.' Kiwi visitors are warned that if you wear thongs you can't lift anything without slipping, your feet will get dirty and smell of stale rubber, and if you kick someone it will hurt you more than it hurts them.

Jets A savoury biscuit made by Arnott's.

juggle-oh Male who services a rotating selection of older women in return for financial benefits.

juggler One who agitates a Lipton's tea bag in a cup of hot water. The 'Lupton's jugglers' commercial has annoyed people on both sides of the Tasman.

Jumbo Small, terrier-like Jimmy Connors dominated tennis in the seventies. 'Come on, Jumbo!' his Kiwi fans used to shout. Visitors may have thought it was an ironic nickname; that is because the existence of Kiwese has been kept secret in all the guide books. Footnote: Connors was supplanted as world number one by Ivan 'Lyndall'.

jun fuzz Fizzy drink with a gin base. Similar to a 'jun slung' or a 'punk jun'.

Jungle Bill's Sounds like a trading post or a chain of restaurants or a nursery rhyme like Grocer Jack's, but in Kiwese this is a Christmas song:

Jungle Bill's, Jungle Bill's
Jungle all the way
Oh what fun . . . etc.

Jupp Orchestra leader Eric Jupp is a well-known
Australian. He did *not* lend his name to the
Kiwese expression, 'I was Jupped' (i.e. cheated,
bilked, swindled), although the derivation is
'E. Jupp', a country on the River Nile with
plenty of sharp merchants and the inscrutable
'Sphunks'.

K

Keir A fairly common surname in Australia, but in
New Zealand it means loving responsibility, as
in the pop classic 'Take Good Keir of My Baby'.

Ken's Cairns. Whereas many Australians call this
northern city Cans, the local Kiwi contingent
call it 'Ken's'. There is in fact no 'Ken' and no
one person owns Cairns.

Kerenga Heppy *Not* a disease but the name of a
street in Auckland where you can buy or contract
almost anything you want. Karangahape Road
has every kind of exotic food, excellent bookshops
and green-grocers, lots of odd stores where you

can buy 'nuck-necks' and 'bruc-a-brek', as well
as 'jums' and 'hilth clubs' where people pump
iron and socialise. The street has a bad reputation
at night and this was supposed to have
contributed to the failure of the Mercury Theatre.
During the day, however, it is an authentic
part of the Asia–Pacific region.

ketch's mutt Glove used by close fielder in
baseball. Not the canine equivalent of a ship's
cat. One of the greatest catchers in baseball
history was Roy Campanella of the Los Angeles
Dodgers. At any auction his mitt would bring a
good price. There are no 'ketch's mutts' in NZ
baseball that would get close.

Ketch-22 You'd have to be crazy to enter the
America's Cup, but you can't win it if you're
crazy. This is a new form of Catch-22. Australian
cynics say the Kiwis will only win the Cup after
21 unsuccessful attempts, with Ketch 22.

ketchup football In America 'ketchup football'
involves the use of violent tactics which result in
the spilling of 'ketchup' (blood). In Kiwese it
is quite different; it simply means the kind of
football you have to play if you are behind on the
scoreboard and have to 'ketch up'. This quite

often — but not always — involves the use of violent tactics.

kettle 'Even at morning tea they have meat' was often said about New Zealand. The cattle, or 'kettle', graze on fine grass and the result, on the table, when all is said and done, is excellent.

Kevin Rock formation, room formed by rocks, cave.

Key Tongue Oz prime minister (a surname not a title). Paul Keating gave voice to republican and amalgamationist sentiments which alarmed older Kiwis. 'Brung beck Muster Minzies!' they wailed.

Kiminy's Supermarket on Bondi Road. Most of the staff and customers are from the Shakies, and it is said that this is where you will hear the purest Kiwese spoken in Australia. You will certainly hear a lot of it.

Kip First name of South African cricket captain, 'Kip Whistles', who is anything but sleepy.

When South Africa was re-admitted to world cricket in 1992, it was under the captaincy of Kepler Wessels, the game's greatest survivor (after Tony Greig).

Kiri Pecker Australian business magnate and owner of Channel Nine, which has provided a steady source of employment for a stream of Kiwis. Who was Brian Henderson's predecessor as the station's newsreader? 'Davud Low'.

kirov A ballet company to some, but a Kiwese expression as well. Some tourists in NZ are reassured when they ask about their baggage and are told 'Ut's been taken kirov'.

kitsch Small boat. Many Kiwese-speakers own a 'kitsch' or a 'smeck' for sailing, fishing or racing. Aucklanders, in particular, are seafaring folk who love a 'rigetta'.

Kittle crusps Kettle Chips are known by this name in Kiwese.

Kitty Lister Not a drunk cat, but an American singer. Ketty Lester was popular in NZ, as are many American country and western singers. One of her biggest hits was 'I'm Gonna Sut Right Down and Write My Sylph a Litter'. This in turn should not be confused with the feline hygiene product kitty litter, which is pronounce['cutty lutter' in Kiwese.

Kiwi Cooee An entertaining and informative newspaper which services the New Zealand community in Australia. English language.

Kiwi–Polish To be of Kiwi–Polish stock is quite rare, as the only Slavs to have migrated to NZ in large numbers are the Yugoes who have distinguished themselves in the wine industry, acting (Bruce Spence), academia (Victor Emeljanow) and both codes of rugby (Frano Botica).

krebs A popular crustacean. Also a sexually transmitted disease said to have been introduced to New Zealand some thirty years before the Treaty of Waitangi by a visit from the Sydney boat *The Active*, skippered by the Rev. Samuel Marsden. No reflection on the character of Maynard G. Krebs is intended. As played by Bob Denver, Krebs was a regular scene-stealer in the popular television series *The Many Loves of Dobie Gillis*.

krupp tuck Type of crossword puzzle, with obscure clues like 'Face-lift for German arms manufacturer'.

L

LA Circumvent reassuringly, soothe, placate: e.g.
'Washington moved swuftly to LA fears that . . .'

Laurie 'Bare' Knuckles Scantily-clad football
personality Laurie Nicholls is becoming a 'cult
fugger' on both sides of the Tasman, thanks to
extensive television coverage, which has restored
the concept of the 'Australasian personality'.
Other football identities to impress throughout
the Antipodes are tiny 'Elf' Langer, Mario
'Finick', 'Tum' Sheens, Trevor 'Gull Muster',
'Much' Healey, Darrell 'Trundle', Dean 'Scuffle
Utty', Brett 'Gold Spunk' and 'Fetty' Vautin.

The Kiwis' favourite player is of course Terry Lamb and they follow 'Maori–Warringah' as a second team.

lear An exhibitionist, a show-off. If Laurence Olivier had been a New Zealander he would have been called a 'mug lear'.

leather A razor strop in Oz is made from leather, but in Kiwese 'leather' is foam produced from shaving cream. It can also be used metaphorically, as in 'Rugby supporters worked themselves into a leather over their idol's exclusion from The Dome Onion.' (Translation: Fans of cartoonist Paul Rigby were upset that his work was not displayed in Wellington's leading newspaper *The Dominion*.)

lessee Renting a flat in Bondi or St Kilda you will find many a Kiwi 'lessee.' The Highland Games in Dunedin attract many 'leds' and 'lessees'. A small man in Kiwese is a 'wee led', while a big girl is a 'bug lessee'.

letter Following, subsequent: e.g. Mormons are known as the 'Letter' Day Saints. In the 'letter' stages of its 'hustory', New Zealand exported more people than sheep.

lex Slack, lackadaisical, unwilling to enforce standards. The Reformation was said to have come about because the clergy were worldly and 'lex'. In more recent times, Australian welfare organisations have been said to be 'lex' about dole conditions.

Licks Boy's name, short for Alexander. Lex Barker and Lex Marinos were popular actors in New Zealand. Not so popular was the villain in *Superman*, played by Gene 'Heckman'. His name? 'Licks' Luther.

lift Departed: e.g. 'They hed a tough and she lift'.

Lit Australian literature is not popular in New Zealand. An exception is the lively, satirical work of Oz novelist 'Kethy Lit', author of *The Llama Parlour* and *Foetal Attraction*. She is more widely read than 'Petrarch' White and 'Crusteena' Stead, possibly because her work is shorter and punchier. Some critics have looked down on Kathy Lette's puns — her jokes, not her legs — because they realise that if verbal

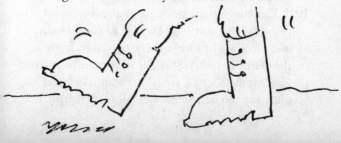

dexterity were given a high rating they would be out of a job.

London The capital of England to Australians, but a boy's name in Kiwese. Only one American president shook hands with NZ Prime Minister Keith Holyoake in the southern hemisphere. His name? Lyndon Baines Johnson, known simply as 'London' to Holyoake insiders.

Love Allman Swedish film star with evangelical name. Liv Ullman starred in *Forty 'Kerretts'*, *Queen 'Crusteena'* and *The 'Immigrants'*.

Lover Pool City west of Sydney named for Colonial Secretary Lord Liverpool. More and more Kiwis are migrating to the west of Sydney from the east of Sydney because of employment opportunities, disproving the myth that all Kiwis are on the (Australian) dole.

luckward Fluid state, freely flowing, soluble, solvent. 'Luckward' assets are those which are readily convertible to 'kesh'.

luft Elevator, boost, evidence of predisposition towards liveliness: e.g. Bowler Richard Hadlee was often said to have extracted 'Luft' from the Basin Reserve. This did not mean he rescued Liza Minnelli's half-sister; it meant the great man got the ball to bounce high off the pitch at

Wellington's premier cricket ground, the Basin Reserve, which sounds like a wilderness area to the uninitiated. Note: Singer Lorna Luft, a product of the marriage between Judy Garland and Sid Luft, has successfully toured New Zealand and Australia.

Lumbar American television personality Rush Limbaugh shocked regulars of the Phil Donahue show when he disagreed with the white-haired liberal, whose show has been 'on the ear' for many years in the Shakies, as well as Australia. 'Lumbar' has so far proved too controversial for the 'region', as K. Lette might say, and his show is not seen regularly here.

lump rust Cars in seaside Oz are affected by 'lump rust', a disconcerting process in which large lumps of rusted metal fall off. In Kiwese, however, a 'lump rust' is supposed to be a sign of masculine effeminacy.

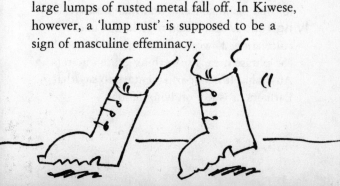

lunch mob Vigilante posse with rope. Said to have abounded in the Wild West of America and the Gold Coast of Australia. There is no record of anyone being 'lunched' in the modern era in NZ.

lung Pink, thick-gilled, large-ribbed fish, usually bought in 'fullets'.

Lunn Popular surname in Oz (author Hugh Lunn, journalist Sarah Lunn etc.), but a girl's first name in Kiwese. Short for Lynette. 'Grey Lunn' is a suburb of Auckland. Lynn is a boy's name in South Australia only.

Lunt Alfred Lunt and Lynn Fontanne were American stage stars who have been forgotten by the public, especially in NZ, where 'lunt' is 'runced' out of clothes in a washing machine.

Lust High-libido composer. 'Frenz Lust' is famous for one piano concerto and many mistresses.

lying fellow Condition of field not under cultivation. Kiwese speakers should note that the phrase means something quite different in Australia. It is unparliamentary to say that Parliament is full of 'lying fellows'.

M

McKennock Person who fixes cars.

Mend Delay *'Road to Mend, Delay'* was a popular
film in NZ, starring 'Bung' Crosby. In 1993
American singer Blossom Dearie appeared at the
'Mend Delay' Entertainment Centre, Auckland.
The original Mandalay is a 'suttee' in Burma.

Menly Sydney suburb. A Kiwi enclave that almost
rivals Bondi. It makes sense, I suppose, to call
Manly 'Menly' as there is more than one man
there.

mere Insubstantial, largely ceremonial political
office. The 'Lord Mere' of Auckland has little

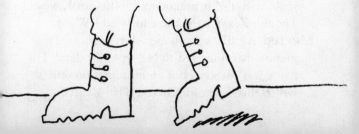

real power and the Town Hall is no longer
'Micca'. It is the same story in Australia. In
Adelaide, for instance, the 'Town Whore' is
impressive and straddles the footpath, but the
Lord Mayor inside does not have to do much.

mess kara Eye make-up. Kara is a popular girl's
name in NZ, and if someone called Kara worked
in a naval officers' dining room, then, well, yes,
she could be called 'Mess Kara'.

mess toughs Large dogs, often ferocious.

Messy Whist Auckland suburb, not an untidy
card game. Contains even more Kiwis than
Bondi, Manly, the Gold Coast, St Kilda or
Cairns. Kiwese is the official language in Massy
West.

Metz First name of fighting Swedish tennis player
Mats Wilander. The Swedes were popular in
Kiwiland, especially 'Bettling Metz', ladies' man
'Stiffen' Edberg, and the baseline fixture
'Endless' Jarryd. Note: The town in Lorraine
spelt M-E-T-Z is pronounced 'Mitts' in Kiwese.
The 'En Zex' fought there in World War I.

Mexted All Black footballer Murray Mexted's
grandfather migrated to NZ from Scotland. His
name was McStead but an immigration official
wrote this down in Kiwese. The Mexteds,

proud Kiwis, have never tried to change the
spelling back to English.

mezzo-balls Along Bondi Road, which is
simultaneously a Jewish and Kiwese stronghold,
matzo balls are a popular foodstuff enjoyed
traditionally by Jews and now increasingly by
Kiwis. In New Zealand itself 'Mezzo-Balls' is a
name given to a man with a high-pitched voice.

Milburn Capital of Victoria. Fewer Kiwis migrate
to 'Milburn' than go to 'Sudney', 'Bruzbane' and
'Ken's'. This is because they play a different
code of football in The Land of the Long White
Posts, and withdrawal symptoms may be too
great. Curiously Perth has a strong Kiwese-
speaking community. Were they there to get
away from New Zealand or football I asked one
couple. 'Both!' they answered.

milton Become liquid in: e.g. 'Butter wouldn't
milton huz mouth'.

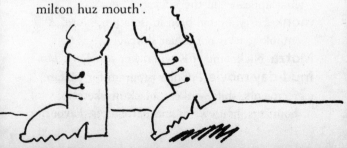

min The male of the species in NZ has evolved to the point where there are 'min's groups' such as MOP ('Min Opposed to Petriarchy') and MUMPS ('Min Understanding Min's Problems'). Some Kiwi women have welcomed these developments while others prefer to get married and have children.

M'lud My hat.

Moll Year Seventeenth century French playwright, author of '*A Fuzzushun un Spite of Hum Sylph*'.

monetary Threatening. Kiwis were scared by Rogernomics.

Money Spouse to Mickey Mouse. Also, a small car. In some hotels the rooms have a lucrative 'money bar', consisting of small overpriced bottles of 'lucker' for which the guests are charged whether they drink them or not.

money-skirt Expensive, fashionable item that first appeared in the 'sucksties'.

monk Furry animal bred in isolation. Note: A 'monk coat' is not a hair shirt.

Motza Nickname of Kiwi cricket star Dick Motz.

mud-day movie Popular program for welfare recipients, shift workers, black marketeers, bouncers, housewives and bartenders. Favourite movies include '*An Affear to Rimimber*', '*A Fear-Will to Arms*', '*The Fearaoh*', '*State Fear*', '*Clear's Knee*' and '*Five Fungus*', also known as '*Operation Sus Hero*' in which James Mason, co-starring with Danielle Derriere, plays a spy who betrays the Allies in World War II. One of the most enjoyable of the 'mud-day movies' is *Until They Sail*, which is actually set in New Zealand, mainly in Christchurch and Wellington. Four sisters, played by Joan Fontaine, Piper Laurie, Jean Simmons and Sandra Dee, share a house and become involved with some American soldiers in World War II. 'I've never seen so many flashing white teeth,' says Jean Simmons when the Yanks arrive. 'We have supper at 6.30,' Joan Fontaine tells one of them. 'Everyone gets tanked in the afternoon because your bars close at six,' observes Paul Newman. As the film was made in 1957, everyone playing a Kiwi tries an English accent.

muddy A large glass of beer. A 'muddy' is only muddy when the beer concerned is Cooper's Ale.

mulch-cow No 'ebbet wars' for this animal. A milch-cow is kept alive, milked, and provides the source for 'dearie' products. During winter they are fed on hay or mulch.

Mullet American feminist Kate Millet was widely read in Wellington in the early seventies.

Mulletry 1. Adherence to the writings of Kate Millet. 2. Knowledge of fishing and filleting. 3. Armed forces, to do with the army: e.g. Ruchard Pape won the Mulletry Middle (M.M.) for bravery in World War II. 4. Slow or sedate: e.g. He bowled medium pace, but ut was a virry mulletry medium.

Mull Hull Bust Row Formerly 'The Dinnison', now an up-market, remodelled pub with bistro, situated near Denison and Mill Hill Roads, Bondi Junction. Formerly a Kiwi hang-out.

mulliner Hat maker.

munce Shred, grind. 'Munce meat' is the basis for many dishes. Combined with 'spur gitty', it is sold by the 'ton'. Also, name of jockey, Chris Munce. Note: In parts of Oz, 'munce' are periods between 28 and 31 days.

munner stroney Soup with a bit of everything in it.

Mush 'L' This comes after Mush 'K' in the Commonwealth Serum Laboratories, where toxic chook food is being analysed. In Kiwese, Mush 'L' is a girl's name. It was immortalised in the Paul McCartney song 'Michelle Ma Belle'.

must Essential ingredient in many NZ harbours is the fog, or 'must', that rolls in almost every day. The mountains also inspire 'must'.

Must Erasure Code name for Kiwi drug boss Terence Clarke. The Mr Asia Syndicate had its headquarters in Bondi until Clarke was rubbed out in a gangland 'culling'.

Musty An old Ray Stevens record which was a 'hut' in the Shakies. The film *'Play Musty for Me'* was also popular more than twenty years ago.

muths 'Muths' are different from 'ligends'. It is a 'muth' that almost all Kiwi males could play international football. It is a 'ligend' that when

they are drunk they clutch their gimpy knees and wail, 'I could have been an All Bleck . . .'

mutton A woollen glove, with holes in the end. Another product from the durable sheep!

muxed merriages Do mixed marriages between New Zealanders and Australians work? There are many successful examples, such as Derryn Hinch and Jacki Weaver. Some Australians find Kiwis are a little melancholic, very serious and rather too inquisitive. The Australian must understand that the cold, harsh weather in En Zed drives people indoors and can be depressing. As there is a village atmosphere in the Shakies, and no convict background, it is considered okay to ask questions. The Kiwi, in turn, often finds the Australian to be crass, volatile and uncaring.

N

nan tucket According to a Shaky legend, Air
New Zealand once offered free travel to America
for any grandmother accompanying a family
of ten, on a so-called 'nan tucket' (source: *Tall
Tales of the Antipodes*, by Perce P. Cassidy).

nicked Swallowed, disposed of, necked.

nicked run Not a stolen base, but a kind of stone
fruit, mid-way between a peach and a 'peer'.

nit Hair accessory in New Zealand, where many
people go to bed wearing a hair net. A 'nit' is
also used to 'ketch' fish and register goals in
soccer. A depressing sight for NZ soccer fans is

to see their goal-keeper 'fushing the ball out from the beck of the nit'. Many expat Kiwis work for Telecom's 'Mobile Nit'.

no one Non-existence or lack of status where victory is concerned. A 'no one' situation denotes that victory is unachievable.

N.R. Peck One When Kiwi Anna Paquin won the Oscar for best supporting actress in *The Piano*, the 'ear waves' in NZ were full of praise for the youngster. They pronounced the little girl's name 'N.R. Peck One' and referred to her parents as her 'peer runts'. Oz speakers should know that this is simply Kiwese pronunciation, and no comment is intended on the size of those described.

null Not existing, a void, zero, blot. When the All Blacks defeated South Australia 99–nil, their coach praised his team's defensive effort. He was 'pleased about the ninety-nine and even more pleased about the null'.

Numb Bun In the early 1970s NZ 'huppies' flocked to Nimbin, the New South Wales capital of sandals, beards and beads. In 1993 the district went through 80,000 syringes. If these were pain-killing or inoculatory needles — and that surely must be the most likely story —

then there are a lot of people in Nimbin with 'numb buns'.

numble Sounds like a sleepy country town in Oz, but it means agile and energetic, as in this nursery rhyme:

Jack be numble
Jack be kwuck
Jack jump over . . . oh no . . .
The candle stuck!

Nun Tin Dough Computer game.

nuptials Japanese wedding.

nutting In Australia this is a sporting term describing the practice of member-crunching, or landing low blows. In Kiwese it is a hobby requiring a ball of wool and two large needles.

N. Yuille There is no travel agent by this name. It is a Kiwese expression meaning something that occurs once a year. Many New Zealanders go to the Gold Coast for 'N. Yuille holidays' and so

locals mistakenly believe they have a travel agent
called N. Yuille.

O

ocker Australian. The term may have disappeared from the Oz lexicon, but it is alive and well in New Zealand. In Australia an 'ocker' belonged to that minority who were geeks or dorks or losers; in the Shakies the expression refers to *all* Australians.

once Facial expression, painful or disapproving grimace. In Oz a 'oncer' is a person who cannot repeat a success, but in NZ a 'oncer' is a dyspeptic complainer.

Once Ton Brand of American cigarette. Also, first name of politician 'Once Ton' Peters, head

of the breakaway New Zealand First Party.
Some believe 'Once Ton' carried more weight as
a National MP; others believe he has spent too
much time at late-night Maori meetings. He
does have, however, like many Kiwis, a rich,
resonant speaking voice. Perhaps the only office
left open for 'Once Ton' is that of President
of Australasia.

One Array Rugby star Wilson Whineray had all
the skills. Despite this, he was called 'Wulson
One Array' in Kiwese.

one doe Glass aperture, often operated by sash
cord: e.g. 'Open the one doe, Bread dear, and lit
some ear un.'

One Free Surname of talk show host seen every
afternoon on NZ television. More of an agony
sister than an agony aunt, Oprah Winfrey was
once the target of an attack by President
Clinton. 'Get one free,' he kept saying.

One Ton Marsalas Large after-dinner drinks?
No, the Kiwese for popular musician Wynton
Marsalis.

open roughed Overt hostility or dispute: e.g.
There was an open roughed between Jum Bolger
and Once Ton Peters, whuch resulted un the
resugnation of the letter.

overhead Rex Not a tall man or a jumping dog,
but shelves in trains and boats and planes.
Kiwese announcers often exhort passengers not
to leave any luggage in the 'overhead Rex'.
Note: Most announcers and travel hosts in
Australia are from the Shakies, so visitors to the
Antipodes are urged to bone up on Kiwese,
regardless of which of the two countries you are
visiting. The lazy tourist who thinks Kiwese
is only spoken in New Zealand will soon get into
difficulties in Australia.

P

peck A light kiss in Oz, but to stuff or load in New Zealand. If a Kiwi says 'I'm pecking a suitcase' it is not a sign of frustration (although it could be).

pedals Sporting equipment operated in circular motion. Canoes or kayaks would be useless without 'pedals'. To be 'up shut creek without a pedal' is to be in an awkward position. Also, nickname of cricket legend 'Sir Ruchard Headley'.

peer Two of a kind. The song 'Send In the Clowns' goes like this in Kiwese:

Uzzent ut ruch
Aren't we a peer . . .

pellet Upper part of mouth; artist's tool.

pendennis South Pacific tree. Very common in
Fiji, the Pandanus can also be seen in New
Zealand and, to a lesser extent, Oz.

pen doubt Developed, resulted, proved itself.
'Thetz how ut pen doubt' = That's how it
panned out. The expression dates from the gold
rush days of the nineteenth 'sin cherie'.

Perce P. Cassidy Courageous, far-sighted
journalist who edited an English language
newspaper on Queensland's Gold Coast. An
avowed enemy of the Tin Ears of Academe, Perce
identified and classified the Kiwese language
at a time when it was held to be non-existent.
Indefatigable chronicler of the idiom of the
people. Author of *Tall Tales of the Antipodes* and
The Divine Comedy of Oceania. An observer of
perspicacity.

petriarchy Kiwis are dominated by their animal
companions. It is not uncommon to see the dog
being fed first and best in a Shakies household.
'Peretz' and other caged birds are popular,
along with 'gunny pugs' and 'Shitland ponies'.

Phar Lap NZ's famous horse was christened 'Philip', but was inaccurately written down as 'Phar Lap' by an Australian racing official who was not well versed in Kiwese. (Source: *Tall Tales of the Antipodes* by Perce P. Cassidy). He 'one' one Melbourne Cup. Film version of the horse's life, a nagiography, was directed by Simon 'Oncer'. There was no sequel, and Wincer disappeared overseas. Other NZ horses did well, like 'High Junks', but there was none with the heart of Phar Lap.

Phlegm US Davis Cup player. Herb Flam was the mainstay of American tennis in the 1950s (*after* the Frank Renouf era). According to Perce P. Cassidy, he was greeted by expectorant crowds in New Zealand.

phonetuc Enthusiastic to the point of obsession. When the 'Prutty Thungs' toured NZ in the 'sucksties' they attracted 'phonetuc' support.

pictoral Chest muscles. Maori warriors seem to have prominent 'picks'.

pigs Small devices for pinning washing on clotheslines.

pippa A girl's name in Oz, but a condiment in Kiwese, usually in tandem with salt.

pissed aside Chemical which terminates insects. 'W.A. Fluck' is a leading manufacturer of pesticides.

pity larceny Not to be confused with compassion fatigue or special pleading, 'pity larceny' is committed by 'crumbs' who go to jail for the offence.

polla-tuck Judicious or advantageous course of action. To praise New Plymouth while in New Plymouth would be the 'polla-tuck' thing to do. Some feel it was not a great day for New Zealand when Rob Muldoon went into 'polla-tucks'.

prophet-shearing Socialism, with overtones of abuse and sadism.

pub lushes Publishers.

puck chez Pictures, paintings, iconography, 'fulm'. *Not* the goal in ice hockey, which would at most be 'chez puck'.

puddle Liquid in expulsion mode.

pug Large, truculent, heavy-breathing animal. 'Puggy' Muldoon once punched a heckler during an election campaign.

pump To procure or act as an agent for a prostitute. In Oz, it is a sexual term.

pundit Affix with small metal shaft: e.g. He pundit on the notice-board.

punk Off-red, flesh-coloured. In politics pink means not quite red, but a 'punk runce' is a startling hair colour in its own right.

pun number Secret code used in the operation of automatic bank teller machines. At a bank you may be asked your 'pun number' before cashing a 'chick'. Note: Never offer a 'chick' to a Kiwi tradesman. They do not understand such customs.

Punter English playwright. Theatre audiences are now called 'the punters' in Australia, but in New Zealand they are known as 'the hats', 'the angels', or the 'pub luck' (because you're lucky to get 'em away from the pub). A well balanced season at a New Zealand theatre would probably consist of *'The Neck'* by Ann Jellicoe, *'The Muddle of the Night'* by Paddy Chayefsky, *'The Keir Taker'* by Harold 'Punter', plus a couple of classic plays by 'Chickov' and 'Bricked'. At Downstage in Wellington you would be likely to see plays from England by authors such as David 'Hear' and Peter 'Knuckles'. Australian plays are not staged in NZ, because of some lingering prejudice among the intelligentsia, but Oz soapies are increasingly popular on television, with *Neighbours* once again the flagship of Australian culture.

puppies A kind of small shellfish. 'Puppy Beach' is popular with Kiwi surfers. Note: Dogs are not allowed on 'Puppy Beach', which is situated south of Yamba in northern New South Wales.

pups High-pitched sounds heard every hour on the radio. 'I'll be beck after the suck suck lock pups,' said a Kiwi announcer at 5.59.

pus Yellow excretion. 'A night out on the pus' is not as bad as it sounds.

pustul Explosive weapon firing bullets.

Puttwater Waterway north of Sydney full of Kiwis in their little motor boats.

putz Down-market venue, lower depths, poor
   standard of accommodation or behaviour. The
   Roxy and the Palladium in New Plymouth were
   notorious 'flea-putz'.

pynchon At the age of 60 or 65, New Zealanders
   can claim the 'pynchon'. Some older people are
   dependent on their 'pynchon chick'.

Q

quist Search, desire, venture. Not to be confused
   with the Oz rhyming slang 'I'm feeling a bit
   Adrian Quist', i.e. pissed. Note: Adrian Quist
   was an Oz Davis Cup star of the 1930s.
qut for life 1. Slogan of anti-smoking campaign.
   2. Tenure at the Queensland University of
   Technology.

R

rear A country of extremes, New Zealand offers
steak in two ways, 'rear' or 'will done'. Do not
be alarmed if a Kiwi philatelist offers to give
you some 'rear stamps'. The term 'rear butt' is
not tautological; it is a Welsh meat dish.

reckon Estimated stage in decline and fall. Eg:
'The economy was in a state of reckon rouen,'
said Mr Douglas.

Rid A Dear Trouble shooter Red Adair worked
for oil companies, and put out many fires on
'rugs' in the Tasman Sea. The film of his life was
called '*Hill Fighters*' and starred big John

Wayne as the diminutive 'A Dear'. In January
1994 'Rid A Dear' announced his retirement.

Ridgey Vee There is plenty of Regional Variation
in Oz speech, as we have seen, and there is just
as much Reggie Vee in the Shakies, only there
they call it 'Ridgey Vee'. Some academics have
tried to deny the extent of 'Ridgey Vee', but
they usually change their minds after a visit to
Otago.

rid litter If you hear a Kiwi saying it is a 'rid
litter day', do not call the RSPCA. They are not
going to drown their kittens but, rather,
celebrate some good news.

Rinoof Sir Frank Renouf represented New Zealand
in the Davis Cup, made a fortune, married Susan
Sangster, lost a fortune, was divorced by Lady
Renouf, and retired. To 'Rinoof' is to experience
life's full cycle, and is the opposite of 'rinugg',
as renege is pronounced in Kiwese.

Rob's mob Followers of NZ Prime Minister
Robert 'Puggy' Muldoon. Insular and aggressive,
they were known as 'Pug Islanders'. Muldoon's
comment 'They've raised the IQ of both
countries' when asked about the large numbers
of Kiwis migrating to Australia remains one

of the finest aphorisms on the subject of trans-Tasman relations.

rough Vigorous, repeated musical passage. Guitarists play 'roughs' on their guitar in rhythm and blues bands. 'Rough' was also the name of a character in *West Side Story*. A member of the Berber people of Morocco would be called a 'rough' in NZ without any malice intended.

round table Panel of Auckland business leaders, such as Michael Fay and Douglas Myers, who advise the government about issues affecting Auckland business leaders.

rub it Noise made by frog.

ruck otter A kind of cheese. Also, a rugby player who scoops up the ball and surfaces with it during mauls.

Rucky May Singer, originally from 'In Zid'. He dominated the scene in 'Seedney' with his powerful, resonant voice, coming from that typical Kiwi asset, a big chest. Ricky May had

more front than Grace Brothers and a lot of
colourful friends.

rug Large truck in more than one section. Driving
your 'rug' down NZ's empty highways can be a
lonely experience. Also means to corrupt or
tamper with, as in 'the vote was rugged' or 'he
was able to rug the poker game'.

Rugby Cartoonist. The black-and-white art of
Paul Rigby has been syndicated in NZ.

rugger Fearless person who works high up on
buildings, cranes or lifts.

rum jungle Short advertising song used in tourism
industry. Since NZ was designated part of the
Pacific Rim they have used this in their
advertising. Proud to be on the 'rum', they have
come up with a lot of catchy jingles, or, as they
put it, 'jungles'.

rum shot Drummers in bands get a different
sound when they hit the edge of their 'sneer'.
This is called a 'rum shot' and is not to be
confused with the historic New South Wales
democratic ideal of 'a free shot of rum for every
man, woman and child'.

runcible Able to be rinsed. This word occurs in
'The Owl and the Pussycat'. Few people know
that it was one of the earliest nursery rhymes

written in Kiwese; they think 'a runcible spoon'
is just a nonsense phrase.

rung 'un Cricket term. Talented late inclusion in
social team. The ABC cricket team was notorious
for its 'rung 'uns', mostly first grade players
who had no connection with the ABC.

rusk Dangerous degree of unpredictability.

rust Joint located between the hand and the arm.
'Tin Dulkar's very rusty' does not mean that
Tendulkar hasn't played for a while; it just
means he uses his wrist a lot. 'Rust Never Sleeps'
is a lubricant slogan, not a hymn to onanism.

rut It's a daily grind for Kiwi lawyers, issuing
'ruts', wearing 'wugs', briefing 'berrusters' and
establishing 'prissy dints'.

ruthm end blues A music idiom believed to
have originated with American guitarist 'Bo
Dudley'. Many Kiwi singers had the 'soul sound'
and fronted bands on both sides of the Tasman.
Unfortunately for them, 'dusco' took over

from R & B. Older supporters became members
of the Tamla—Mozart generation and switched
to classical music. For Kiwi descendants of Bo
Diddley it was the clubs or a job.

S

scuffle Rough-as-bags home-made music. Skiffle
groups used washboards and T-chests and had
some big hits in the fifties, such as 'My Old
Man's a Dustman' (Lonnie Donegan). Now, most
'scuffle' musicians are down-at-heel buskers,
singing songs by Bob 'Dull 'un' and John 'Linen'
in the subways of Antipodean cities. Ninety
per cent of the buskers in Australia are Kiwis,
and so are ninety per cent of the buskers in
New Zealand.

scrum Diaphanous curtain used to create poetic
moments in stage productions. Joshua Logan

used a scrim in his Broadway production of *South Pacific*, a knock-off of which toured the actual 'South Pacufuc'. Note: For effective use of the 'scrum' the lighting must be 'dumb'.

scrum shenks One who 'shenks' in scrums. Rugby term (derogatory).

scum 'Dearie' product. Diet-conscious Kiwis drink 'scum mulk'.

scupper Leader, boss, 'kept in', head honcho, number one, chief: e.g. 'In Zid's 1987 America's Cup Challenge was scuppered by Chrus Duckson.'

scuttle Nine-pin, butt, defeat, rout. The most popular form of skittles today is ten-pin bowling. 'Utz not all beer and scuttles un the Navy,' recruits are warned. At Pearl Harbor the US Fleet was 'scuttled'.

secks Plural of sack. If a Kiwese-speaker talks about 'ruck sex' do not be confused. This is not the outcome when rugby is played in co-ed schools. 'Ruck secks' is the plural of ruck sack.

sect A small group of Kiwis say 'I've been sect' when they are dismissed. The majority say, 'I've been govern the fluck.' Ozzified Kiwis say, 'I've been fired.'

Seedney Like 'Breeze Bun' this is a form of
Reverse Kiwese practised by En Zedders living
in NZ. It refers to the 'buggest suttee' in 'The
Lend of the Ockers' and is an attempt to
poke a bit of harmless fun at the Australian
accent. *See* **Sudney**.

set alight The airwaves in NZ were profoundly
affected by the advent of Sky TV and Cable
News Network, whereby everything came 'live
via set alight'. A bonus for the Kiwis is the
number of Australian events that are telecast live.

Sex A store in Auckland. UK novelist Shirley
Conran and her protegé Julie Burchill claim to
have pioneered the Sex and Shopping novel,
which appeals to the cruder instincts of their
readers. Sex and shopping have always gone
together in Auckland, however, since Sak's Fifth
Avenue opened a branch there.

Shaky Isles New Zealanders prefer to think of
themselves as living in The Land of the Long

White Cloud. 'Shaky Isles' is largely an
Australian invention, and is a reference to NZ's
seismic heritage. En Zedders do not like this
nickname, particularly when it is pronounced
'Shakey Oils' by an Oz-speaker. Curiously, they
do not seem to mind being called Pig Islanders,
a reference to the large number of grunters let
loose on North and South Island many years
ago. Note: If a South African calls a New
Zealander a 'nosey porker' it is because they are
snooping; no connection with the 'Pig Island'
tag is intended.

shearing Splitting the rent of an apartment: e.g.
I'm shearing a flet with Bivan and Hither.

sheep-shearing Agrarian socialism with
overtones of bestiality. There is a Depression-era
joke at the expense of the Kiwi accent that
tells of an Australian down on his luck in the
Shakies. He asks a farmer if there is any chance
of a bit of sheep-shearing. 'Oh no,' answers
the farmer. 'I'm not shearing any of these prutty
ones. You go and find your own sheep.'

sheer drop Stock market crash. In early 1987
there was a 'sheer price rise', but in October of
that year the radio headlines in NZ announced a

'sheer drop'. Note: 'Stocks and sheers' are not
to be confused with sheer stockings.

shekel Handcuff. Often used in the phrase
'Breaking the shekels' which has become a
cricket cliché. The phrase 'ram shekel' refers to
the now discredited practice of handcuffing a
sheep to a fence post for the purposes of abuse.
No case has been proven since an incident of
'ram shekel' in Wanganui in 1949, but some
observers believe it still goes on. In Australia
'ramshackle' has none of these connotations and
it is possible to refer to shearers' quarters as
ramshackle without any suggestive imputation.

shenk Expel gas (rare).

Shilley Surname of poet. Also popular girl's first
name in NZ, either in its own right or as a
contraction of Michelle.

shopping lust Number of items to be bought,
set out on a piece of paper.

shrump Crustacean. What Americans would call a 'pron'. In New Zealand a popular seafood dish is 'shrump cellared'.

shrunk Psychiatrist.

shun Avoiding 'shun soreness' is very difficult for soccer players. The softer ground in NZ is kinder to the shins, but when they come to Australia Kiwi players find the harder ground and generally inhospitable conditions gives them 'shun soreness'. Similarly, cricketers find the bounce higher in the land of Oz and suffer many 'broken fungus'.

shut ketches Short pants (derogatory).

sickened class Despite the country's amazing record of success in music, one rock critic claimed that Crowded House was typical of NZ — 'et the top of the sickened class'. Note: The term 'sickened class sutter zen' is only rarely applied to islanders in Kiwese.

sid Said, related, spoke: e.g. I'm Tid, he sid.

sin cherie One hundred, as in Martin Crowe's 'sin cherie'. The nineteenth 'sin cherie' lasted from 1801 to 1900, during which New Zealand was settled by Europeans who worked hard to establish towns and farms.

Sinner Racing car driver. 'Earton Sinner' was
popular among Sky-Channelling Kiwi expats.
'Formula One' describes the class of car, and does
not mean routine victory. An 'Undy' car is in
another class.

sin to meet her One-hundredth of a metre.

sinus One who engages in science. One of the few
words to be pronounced similarly on both sides
of the 'Tezman'.

sivun sickened delay Talk-back radio has a
seven second delay mechanism so that hoax calls
can be screened out. Some visitors have claimed
that New Zealand is on seven second delay,
a variation on the set-your-watches-back-twenty-
years nonsense of earlier days. The pace of
Dunedin is slower than the pace of Sydney, but
this is only to be expected, given the population
difference.

six Sex: e.g. What do men want? 'Six! They ixpict
ut all the time,' sid an undugnant Hither. An

Australian visitor once asked a New Zealand farmer, 'What do you do about six?' In response the farmer gave a guilty look and said, 'I feed the sheep first . . .'

skier Threat of danger: e.g. 'The dollar's dive threw a skier unto the money market.'

skull A talent, an ability: e.g. 'Tilly Sever Less was en ector of enormous skull,' sid Bivan.

Slums The ghetto-like conditions under which women had to play tennis in the 1970s were changed by a major sponsor, Virginia 'Slums', a brand of cigarette. Although Kiwi women tried hard to qualify for the 'Slums', they failed. No En Zedder has made it to the top ten in women's tennis. Ironically, the slogan for Virginia Slims was 'You've come a long way, baby'.

sluts Some squinty-eyed Australians are called 'slits' as an affectionate nickname. Sophisticated Kiwis know their limitations and do not use this term as it could cause offence.

sneer Trap. In modern, enlightened New Zealand snares are used to trap birds so they can be tagged and released back into the wild kingdom.

Snill Peter Snell won Olympic gold for NZ in the 800 metres.

some petty coe Italian words to make it into
Kiwese include simpatico, patina ('pet unner')
and spaghetti ('spur gitty').

sons In Kiwese theology the seven 'diddley sons'
are greed, gluttony, pride, lust etc.

spear Extra or emergency substitute: e.g. 'spear
tyre'. Do not be alarmed if a Kiwi says, 'I've got
a spear in the boot.'

spear rub Lovers of pork enjoy eating 'spear rub'.
Also name of English magazine. Not to be
confused with manhood ceremony in Australian
Aboriginal corroboree, in which a spear is
rubbed across the chest of the aspirant.

S. Picked Outlook, view from, especially of house.
Kiwi visitors should note that 'southerly aspect'
in an Oz real estate ad often means 'cold'.
Conversely, the Oz settler in NZ should be
warned if told of a 'whist early S. Picked' to a
house. This does not just mean 'westerly aspect';

it also means that the aspect is cold, windy and wet.

spill 1. Tour of duty: e.g. Headley came beck for a sickened spill. 2. Rest, pause: e.g. They decided to spill Headley from the team for the sickened Tist. 3. Nominate letters in sequence: e.g. High school students can't even spill 'coffee'. 4. Magical thrall: e.g. I put a spill on you. 5. Title of film: e.g. *Spillbound* was a Hutchcock movie whuch starred Ungared Bergman.

Splut Inz Pop group whose name derived from the fact that they had left the Shakies, or 'splut In Zid'. When they left Bondi they changed their name, in honour of living conditions there, to Crowded House. Crowded House had a lot of 'huts'.

Sprungboks Relations between South Africa and New Zealand suffered when the Springboks made a meal of the 'All Blex' at 'Eden Pork'. Now called The Proteas, the South Africans are trying to demonstrate that they can get their race relations up to NZ's level. Often lumped together as rugby-mad colonials, there are in fact large differences between the two countries.

Spunks Boxers. The two brothers, Michael and
  Leon Spinks, dominated Sky TV heavyweight
  matches in the 1980s. Both became world
  champions and heroes to the Kiwi expats who
  gathered in Manly pubs for a glass of Kiwi
  Lager, a game of pool and a stoush on the screen.

SQ Off-centre, awry. It was the fashion for
  Australian Labor politicians to wear their ties
  askew as a sign that they were not toffs. This
  was especially affected by long-time Labor Leader
  Bert Evatt. Kiwi Labor Leaders of the period,
  Peter Fraser and Walter Nash, however, would
  never dream of appearing in public with their
  ties 'SQ'.

steer Small raised platform, usually in a series. If
  you hear a Kiwi say 'I'm going up the steers' it
  does not mean he has forsaken sheep. Many
  buildings in Wellington only have one 'flight of

steers' because their height is restricted to two
storeys.

stetustuc Folk tale in modern idiom. Many of
these myths and legends begin 'Nearly one in
every three . . .'

Stiffen Attractive Kiwi girls in Queensland usually
end up working for 'Stiffen', the hairdressing
chain founded by Stefan Ackerie. With its key-
hole shaped entrance revealing its charismatic
staff, 'Stiffen' is a feature of most shopping
centres in the Sunshine State.

stucky-beak Over-inquisitive person. Kiwis are a
naturally curious species, so if they call someone
a 'stucky-beak' it must be a very severe case
of long-nosing.

stuff Corpse. At the Auckland morgue, if you
really want to, you can wait around the back
and watch the police 'de-lover a stuff'. A 'stuff-
up' is a rare form of necrophilia pioneered by
Nelson Rockefeller and Sir Billy Snedden.

Stung Pop star, real name Gordon Sumner. Some
wiseacres have said that NZ is behind the times
and that by the time Sting gets there he is
'Stung'. This is ridiculous. If NZ were indeed
behind the times, i.e. unpolluted and with no

drugs or violent crime etc., then people would be
queueing up to go there.

suck Bed-ridden, not well.

sucksties Libertarian decade between 1960 and
1970 which was said to have shaken up a
previously conservative New Zealand and caused
the mass migration that led to Kiwese expatriate
culture. Student revolt and 'wummun's lubbers'
were apparently all the go at Wellington
University. It was also a decade in which
islanders started to migrate to the Shakies and
the wine industry really got going. The 'Sin Sir'
relaxed his grip and '*Ulusses*' was screened
'unsinsired' to general indifference. Crime,
promiscuity and violence have been blamed on
the 'sucksties' but according to Greg McGee all
the decade did was add two inches to farmers'
sidelevers.

Sudney Capital of New South Wales, the largest
'suttee' in Australasia, and both a Mecca and a

target for the average En Zedder. Once
outrageously described as a congenial meeting
place for Kiwis on the way up and Poms on the
way down, Sydney is now host to any number
of rich and successful Brits and about 100,000
struggling migrants from the Shaky Isles. The
cheerful Sydneysiders know that all the top jobs
go to non-Sydneysiders and they accept this
with good grace. From his office high in the
State Office Block, New South Wales Premier
John Fahey can see all the major institutions of
Sydney (Opera House, Australian Museum etc.)
that are controlled by his fellow Kiwis, and
reflect that a few years ago they were all run by
Poms, Americans or Europeans.

sulk A pouting, gorgeous Wanganui girl once
said, 'You can't be too ruch, too thun, or hev
too many sulk blouses.'

sull 1. Ledge, shelf of window, as in 'one doe sull'.
2. Diminutive or nickname of NZ novelist Sylvia
Ashton-Warner, who is likely to be greeted
'Hi, Sull' in her informal native land.

summer Heat, retain heat at level temperature,
as in the cooking instruction, 'Boil the water,
put the yems un, end then summer for tin
munnets.'

Summons Daytime aerobics king 'Ruchard Summons' is not to be confused with football great Arthur Summons. Both keep fit, but any similarity of orientation ends there.

'Sump Pool Simon' Kiwese nursery rhyme about a careless mechanic.

Sun Agog Great balls of fire? Not really. NZ Jews go to the 'sun agog' on 'setter day'. The synagogue is presided over by a 'Rebb Eye'. Most famous Kiwi Jew: Eric Baume, the original Beast on Channel Seven's long-running 'Beauty and the Beast'. Most people thought he was English, with his Broadcaster's Voice and expensive tailoring. Are NZ Jews Anglicised? Certainly, Yom Kippur has become 'Yom Cuppa'.

sun bun Penal area, originally to allow ice hockey players a chance to cool down. Vigorous Kiwi great Kurt Sorensen spent quite a bit of time in the 'sun bun' during his long and illustrious career in football. Note: In Australia, to 'sun your buns' means to indulge in nude bathing.

sunders Charcoal-like material used in the manufacture of running tracks at the time of the Christchurch Games. Also, short for Cinderella.

sungers Not sausages, singers! Some of the many Kiwi singers to enliven Australia are Kevin Borich, Jenny Morris, Johnny Rebb and Margaret Urlich.

'sunk the buzz mark!' War films are popular with Kiwis everywhere. Apart from *Sink the Bismarck*, starring 'Kin' More and Dana 'One Ter', other favourites include *'Bettle of Bruttan'* and *'Weir Eagles Deer'*. Reverse Kiwese expats like *'The Gins of Navarone'* and *'Pucker Lips Now'*.

sunny cull Sceptical. Nothing to do with shooting animals in daylight.

Sunt Peter New Zealand's wartime Prime Minister Peter Fraser was widely revered and known to some as 'St Peter' because of his grave and charismatic mien. An effective speaker with a neutral accent, he spoke of 'peace' at the 1945 San Francisco Conference, while the Australian delegate, Dr H.V. Evatt, spoke of 'pace'. 'Sunt Peter's' aides, however, left no one in any doubt that New Zealanders spoke in a very 'dustunctuv dial licked'. Curiously, none of the guide books or social histories of New Zealand mention the development of modern Kiwese.

Supermex Paul McNamee and Peter McNamara, the two Macs, won the Wimbledon tennis doubles in 1980. They were known as the 'Supermex' in New Zealand. In the USA, the term refers to golfer Lee Trevino, who hails from south of the Rio Grande. Note: 'Bug Mex' are sold in Kiwese-speaking branches of McDonald's.

supper Connoisseurs of NZ's many fine wines tend to be 'suppers' rather than gulpers. Judges, alas, have to be 'sputters'.

surrep This is not short for surreptitious. 'Surrep' is a thick, sweet liquid usually poured on pancakes. Golden Syrup is very popular in Australia, while in the Shakies maple 'surrep' holds sway. 'Surruptutious' does not normally

mean sticky-fingered in Kiwese, although when
applied to pick-pockets it does.

'sut stullness' Reactionary schools policy
denounced by Wellington educationist F.L.
Combs. He was protesting against the stultifying
practice of merely ordering children to sit still
in class.

suttee Many rural and islander Kiwis have left
home and thrown themselves on the pyres of
'suttees' like Auckland and 'Sudney'.

Sutter One of the streets of San Francisco, named
after Tom Sutter, a pioneer. In Kiwese, however,
it means easy catch, especially at cricket.
'Crowe muffed a Sutter' means Crowe dropped
the ball, not that he interfered with a member
of a distinguished Californian family.

'swab the dicks' A female Oz recruit to the NZ
Navy may be taken aback if asked to carry out
this instruction or, indeed, 'to run some chicks
on the radar'. Seabound sailors may be called
SWODs, or Sailors Without DUKWS. If asked
for 'six', then 'Six what?' is a legitimate reply.
'Frugget' means small ship, so there is no cause
for offence there, at least.

sylph-promoter Diet queen who appears in
women's magazines. 'Ginny' Craig is a 'sylph-
promoter'.

symmetry Rows of neat crosses marking graves
are a feature of most cemeteries. In Australia,
the cemetery is usually on the outskirts of town
and is known colloquially as 'the bone orchard'.
In Kiwiland the arc of life and death ends in
'the symmetry'.

Synnot Ruling body in ancient Rome. As an NZ
teacher would say 'Sus hero was the finest
speaker in the Synnot.' Apart from Cicero, the
Senate was famous as the place where Julius
Caesar was 'culled'.

T

take your puck Exercise your freedom of choice.
  In Kiwese a 'puck' is also a digging implement,
  but not an ice hockey accessory.

techs The goods and services 'techs' was devised
  to make sure those who operated on the black
  market paid their taxes. Many of the black
  marketeers in Australia are Kiwis who are always
  paid in 'cesh' and have a strong aversion to
  'benks' (the Kiwese for a teller is 'Attila').
  Ironically, voters in Australia turned against the
  GST because of its failure in New Zealand,

where the black market is strongly entrenched
and run by experts.

Tek A toothbrush in Oz, but a small nail in
Kiwese.

tend After a few days on Bondi Beach the pale
Kiwi visitor will soon be 'tend'.

ten dory In New Zealand, an Indian style of
cooking usually involving a clay oven. In Oz,
'ten dory' is a big order at the fish market.

Tenure Girl's name. In Australia 'Tenure'
Halesworth was the pin-up of discerning males
in the 1950s, who watched her with interest on
ABC TV. In New Zealand a phenomenon of
the 1980s was the Public March to get the
country moving. It was led by Tanya Harris,
who had a great success and became a media
star. 'Tenure! Tenure!' cried the crowd, which
was, paradoxically, marching in protest against
trade unions and public servants with tenure.
'Tenure' Harris had faded from public view by
the end of the 1980s.

text Levied by the government. 'I'm being text
out of house and home' and 'Cars are too heavily
text in thus country' are common complaints
by Kiwis. They will have you believe that even a
bus ticket is 'text'.

the earring of grievances Is it like The Sword
of Honour or The Bluebird of Happiness or The
Bay of Plenty? Is it a Maori talisman? No, it
isn't. The Earring of Grievances is a process that
happens on talk-back radio.

The lays of our Dave After a stomach upset
and the loss of office, NZ Prime Minister David
'No Nukes' Lange had time to catch up on
his love life and ended up marrying his secretary.
This was all 'grust to the mull' for the 'In Zid'
press, who chronicled the big man's doings in
what he complained was a soap opera style. It
looks as if *The Days of Our Lives* has been replaced
by *The Lays of Our Dave*, he observed. Dave
was soundly ticked off by the Oz media for this
statement, but whether on the grounds that
it was off-colour or clever was not made clear.

tick knuckle Applied science is taught at NZ's
many excellent 'tick knuckle' colleges. Employers
in Australia have been impressed by the high

level of 'tick knuckle skulls' demonstrated by their Kiwese-speaking recruits.

Ticks–Micks Spicily flavoured food influenced by the South Texas–North Mexico axis. 'Ticks–Micks' food is more readily available in Auckland than in Invercargill.

Tilly Sever Less Actor Telly Savalas was a popular hit in NZ with 'Kojak'. His catch phrase 'Who loves ya, baby?' never caught on with older Kiwis.

Tim Pissed Shakespearean play set on island.

tin since Ten cents.

tips The tepid baths in Auckland.

Tit Offensive Off-colour Oz term devised by sardonic observers of the night-club scene in St Kilda. It refers to the invasion of Kiwi strippers in the 1980s.

tough Fight, disagreement, spat. A 'butt of a tough' is a minor disagreement. A 'lover's tough' is a light quarrel between people in love.

trekkies Cult costume worn by Kiwis shopping in Bondi Road. They all wear the lower half of an old track suit. The term 'trekkies' is not to be confused with Boer pioneers or fans of old TV shows.

Trucks Dish-washing liquid. Trix was one of the early 'luckward' detergents.

Trupple 'E' Capital of 'Lubya'.

Trupple 'J' Radio station which employs a healthy quota of Kiwis.

trussed Romantic rendezvous. A lovers' tryst is an appointment made with a beating heart. If, however, you hear a Kiwi say, 'My lover's trussed', it means the liver part of the body has been tightly bandaged. In this case there are no romantic connotations.

tucker Heart: e.g. The way to a man's tucker uz through huz stomach. NZ football teams are so huge and fearsome that opposing players need plenty of 'tucker'. Conversely, when a former All Black signed up with a Sydney club his performances were criticised for being a bit light-on in the ticker department.

Tucker-tick *Not* a restaurant credit system but a booking agency for buying theatre tickets at full price plus fee ('Half-Tucks' offers a fifty per cent discount). Ticketek's predecessor was Computicket, run by Kiwi entrepreneur Harry M. Miller.

Tumbarumba Dashing Kiwi singer Johnny Devlin, the 'Napier Rapier' and a former 'Mr West Coast', had a hit in 1964 with 'Stomp the Tumbarumba', a dance record believed to be based on a saw-miller's pavane. Johnny thought he was saying 'Timber Rhumba' and that the song was full of 'logger rhythms'. He was surprised to find he had put Tumbarumba — a place he had never heard of — on the map. Tumbarumba is today a thriving town where the main export is, you guessed it, wood. (Sources: NSW Forestry Commission Annual Report, *Myths and Legends of the Bombala Shire*, by Perce P. Cassidy).

Tum Fun Not a sensuous meal but a pop singer. 'Tum Fun' wrote 'A Frection Too Much Fruction' and was for a time the domestic partner of 'Gritter Skecky'. His brother, Neil Finn, is also a pop musician.

Tum Illiott NZ-born actor who played the Fred Hollows character in *GP* and the Lachlan Macquarie character in *Macquarie*.

Tummy Euro Pop singer, female. Not to be confused with Euro Tummy, a stomach upset Kiwis get in Europe, where lamb is cooked differently and cakes have chunks of fruit. Timi Yuro had many 'huts' in New Zealand in the 'sucksties'.

Tum-Thames A chocolate-coated 'busket' made by Arnott's. For the sweet-toothed Kiwi a steady stream of Tim-Tams is often the go.

Tupper Wife of US Vice-President Al Gore, Tipper Gore has campaigned to clean up pop music. She could have as big an effect on NZ culture as any US political figure in history.

tupper cull Not an assassination plot, but a prototype. Brian Henderson was a 'tupper cull' Kiwi until he trained himself to say 'typical'.

tupping Gratuities are not generally sought by hotel staff in NZ.

turning a truck A strong component in Australia's burgeoning prostitution industry are

Kiwis, who function as 'pumps' and sluts.
Turning a trick enables the 'six workers' to keep
up drug habits and, in some cases, support
'cuds'.

Tut! Tut! The cry heard at strip-tease shows as
two good reasons to go are revealed. Note 1:
Although *all* bouncers at these clubs are New
Zealanders it is not because of any law requiring
this. Note 2: Kiwi visitors should be told that
'tut tut' is a reproving — not orgiastic — cry in
Oz.

twin tees Not a golf course but the 20-29 age
range at which many Kiwis become expats. En
Zedders in their teens are mostly at school,
while those in their thirties and forties tend to
'merry' and 'sittle down'. Bondi, Manly and St
Kilda are full of Kiwese speakers in their 'mud
twin tees'.

U

Ulcer Girl's name. New Zealand has never produced swimmers of the calibre of Jon and 'Ulcer' Konrads.

Umbarella Mythical, beautiful coastal town in Australia, heavily populated with Kiwis. As Perce P. Cassidy has noted, 'If it's warm and wet with a good view, they'll be there, the silver fern on the golden sand, the long white cloud over the deep blue sea. They always pick the best spot!'

Undies A group of islands in the Caribbean. New Zealand defeated the 'Whist Undies' in a cricket

series in 1980. In Oz, 'Reg Grundies' is rhyming slang for undies. The fact that TV producer Reg Grundy lives in the Caribbean is a minor irony.

Ung. Lut. English Literature, or Eng. Lit., is studied in NZ schools and universities, often with more thoroughness and reverence than it is in Australia. 'Coupling' and 'Duckens' are favourites, of course, along with 'Shilley', 'H.G. Wills', Charles Lamb (naturally), John Stuart 'Mull' and Walter 'de la Meer'.

V

Vet-69 Although many jokes are made about NZ veterinarians and their 'six life', this isn't one of them. 'Vet-69' is a brand of 'whusky'.

W

Walter Plunge When an actor does not want to appear in the program he is usually listed as Walter Plinge, a traditional theatrical pseudonym used all over the English-speaking world. In Kiwese this is 'Walter Plunge' and does *not* imply a downward spiral in the actor's career; quite often the anonymous performer will be famous.

weary Anxious to avoid, suspicious: e.g. 'New Zealanders are weary of chicks,' sid Hither.

weir Drape about the person: e.g. 'I hevvunt got a thung to weir!' (NZ-born NSW Premier John

Fahey, on declining invitation to lead Gay
Mardi Gras parade).

weir and tier Physical depreciation, as in the
phrase 'normal weir and tier'. Camberg's Carpets
at Bondi Junction employed a lot of Kiwis,
whose standard gambit was to say, 'Thus carpet
wul last tin years, assuming normal weir and
tier.' The expression, 'He'd never get a job at
Camberg's' applies to those macho Kiwis who
overestimate the length of their prowess.

Whist Munster Ebby Church in London
favoured by Kiwi tourists. They also like 'Bug
Bin', the 'White Cloughs of Dover', 'N.
Hethaway's Cottage' and 'Stone Hinge'.

Who Deers Ones Film about SAS commandoes
wiping out terrorists, starred Judy Davis and
was not a hit in Australia. Released in the
Shakies as *Who Deers Ones*, it was supposed to be
based on the motto *Who Dares Wins* and was
reputed to be trying to cash in on post-Falklands
euphoria.

will fear Historically, NZ is a welfare state, with
social security 'from the cot to the rot'.
Unemployment is high in the Shakies, with
many young people on 'will fear'.

Willies Boots, said to have been inspired by the Duke of Wellington. One Kiwi preferred to work at a farm where boots were supplied free. 'This place guvs me the willies,' he said.

Winsday Third day of the working week. Racing day in many parts of Australasia.

winton Embarked upon. 'He winton a bunge' = He went on a binge. Note: Winton is a town in Queensland. It is pronounced 'One Ton' by Kiwis and North Queenslanders.

wit Damp, moist, sodden. Opposite of 'dry'. A soaking fishing trap is a 'wit nit'. Stolid pol Ruth Richardson was not a Tory 'wit'.

wither Sheep with inadequate genitalia.

Won A Pig City in Canada. Relations between New Zealand and 'Kenneda' have always been cordial, but they became especially close after the Canadians beat Wales at rugby in 1993 at 'Carduff'. Any self-respecting Kiwi 'Brussels' at the idea that the Welsh were not trying.

world footnotes The Antipodes used to be regarded as footnotes to the world, with no distinctive culture or idiom and no real contribution to make. To be mentioned or singled out meant that you had done something wrong or were being criticised unjustly. Very few tourists ventured 'down under'. By the nineties, however, Australia had a large tourist industry, employing half a million people. Nearly half of these were New Zealanders.

wreck of lemb A popular dish. NZ lamb is so good that you can ask for it to be done 'medium rear'.

wrist arrant Café, eating and drinking establishment. There is a café in Auckland called An Eating and Drinking Establishment.

Wump Lead singer in rock band. Wump and his Werbles toured NZ in the 'sucksties'. In later times, in Kiwese, a 'wump' is someone who does not play rugby, sail a yacht, have millions in the bank and talk all the time (derived from whimper).

X

X. Trevor Ghent Big spender, with big 'shopping lust'.

Y

yefta Not a trade agreement but a contraction of
'You have to': e.g. 'Yefta charge full price for all
the spishels, Lunda,' sid Jeckie. 'Yafta' is the
Oz equivalent; 'Yifta' is Ethiopian.

Z

zid The last letter in the 'elphabit'. Because 'zid' occurs in New Zealand, Kiwis are said to be quick to spot a zee on a page.

zup Nil, no score, 'zulch'. Kiwi expatriates would like nothing better than to see their beloved 'All Blex' defeat Australia 'three-zup' at Brisbane's famous 'Belly More'.

zut Pimple, or, as they say in Kiwese, 'pump pull'. 'Zut alors!' is the Frankie (French Kiwese) for 'I have found a pimple!' but that, as they say, is a whole new ball game.